INFORMATION
TECHNOLOGY
AUDIT
HANDBOOK

DOUG DAYTON

PRENTICE HALL
Englewood Cliffs, New Jersey 07632

Library of Congress Cataloging in Publication Data

Dayton, Doug.
    Information technology audit handbook / Douglas Dayton.
        p.   cm.
    Includes index.
    ISBN 0–13–614314–8
    1. Information technology—Management—Handbooks, manuals, etc.
    I. Title.
    T58.64.D378   1997
    004'.068—dc21

96–40197
CIP

This publication is designed to provide accurate and authoritative information in regard to the subject matter covered. It is sold with the understanding that the publisher is not engaged in rendering legal, accounting, or other professional service. If legal advice or other expert assistance is required, the services of a competent professional person should be sought.

Printed in the United States of America

10 9 8 7 6 5 4 3 2

ATTENTION: CORPORATIONS AND SCHOOLS

Prentice Hall books are available at quantity discounts with bulk purchase for educational, business, or sales promotional use. For information, please write to: Prentice Hall Career & Personal Development Special Sales, 240 Frisch Court, Paramus, NJ 07652. Please supply: title of book, ISBN, quantity, how the book will be used, date needed.

PRENTICE HALL
Career & Personal Development
Englewood Cliffs, NJ 07632
A Simon & Schuster Company

On the World Wide Web at http://www.phdirect.com

Prentice Hall International (UK) Limited, *London*
Prentice Hall of Australia Pty. Limited, *Sydney*
Prentice Hall Canada, Inc., *Toronto*
Prentice Hall Hispanoamericana, S.A., *Mexico*
Prentice Hall of India Private Limited, *New Delhi*
Prentice Hall of Japan, Inc., *Tokyo*
Simon & Schuster Asia Pte. Ltd., *Singapore*
Editora Prentice Hall do Brasil, Ltda., *Rio de Janeiro*

Doug Dayton formed Dayton Associates in May of 1985. Dayton Associates provides strategic Information Technology consulting services and Client-Centered™ Training seminars. Before becoming a consultant, Dayton worked as a marketing representative for IBM's General Systems Division, and managed Sales and Contract Support for Microsoft's OEM Division.

Over the last 12 years, Dayton has been involved with a broad range of consulting projects, including strategic planning and business development consulting, technical evaluations of software companies for investment firms, analysis of emerging computer markets, and senior management coaching.

His clients include: the Canadian Government, Atlantis Aerospace, Corum Group, Delrina Technologies, Digital, Escalator Handrail Company, Futurus, Great Plains Software, J.H. Whitney, Liant Software, Maddocks Systems, Microsoft, NORDX/Cable Design Technologies, Peachtree Software, Physician Micro Systems, Inc., RealWorld Corp., Saros Corp., SBT Corp., Solomon Software, Sygenex, The Executive Committee, U.S. Micro Net and many other technology-driven organizations.

Dayton is the author of *Computer Solutions for Business,* from Microsoft Press, *Selling Microsoft,* from Adams Publishing, and has published over one hundred articles and reference books on computer technologies for *Byte, Computers in Accounting, Computer Reseller News, Connect, Database Advisor, LAN Times, The Office, PC Week, PC Magazine* and *Inst. Information.* He is a frequent speaker at computer industry events, and is a member of the Washington Software Association.

DEDICATION

This book is dedicated to Terry Smith, and to my Mother.

ACKNOWLEDGMENTS

I would like to thank Eugene Brissie and Susan McDermott at Prentice Hall for their help and support on this project.

CONTENTS

CHAPTER 1
MANAGING INFORMATION TECHNOLOGY

CHAPTER 2
THE IMPACT OF EMERGING TECHNOLOGIES

CHAPTER 3
EVOLVING SYSTEMS ARCHITECTURE

CHAPTER 4

STRATEGIC BUSINESS AUDIT WORKSHEETS

CHAPTER 5
INFORMATION SYSTEMS AUDIT WORKSHEETS

CHAPTER 6
EVALUATING NEW TECHNOLOGIES

CHAPTER 7

SECURITY, ORGANIZATION, AND DOCUMENTATION

CHAPTER 8

INFORMATION TECHNOLOGY BUDGETS

CHAPTER 9

REENGINEERING IT SYSTEMS

CHAPTER 10
RECRUITING AND EVALUATING TECHNICAL PERSONNEL

CHAPTER 11
MANAGING AND TRAINING TECHNICAL PERSONNEL

CHAPTER 12
WORKING WITH CONSULTANTS

CHAPTER 13
CALL TO ACTION!

INTRODUCTION

Twenty years ago, most businesses were excited about the opportunity to automate their organizations. There was a tacit belief that automation would improve operations, and that automation would help organizations contain operating costs.

When studies revealed that many companies were in fact not experiencing these benefits, businesses began to look at information technology (IT) spending more critically.

Although IT managers were often unable to demonstrate hard cost savings based on reductions in personnel and improved operating efficiencies, they were able to articulate indirect benefits based on improving corporate decision making and improving competitiveness. Since it is almost impossible to quantify the value of these indirect benefits, the jury is still out on whether these benefits actually justified corporate IT budgets over the last 35 years.

MANAGING IT COSTS

IT spending has increased about 6% per year since 1960, with the exception of 1985, when it declined slightly. The pause in 1985 may be attributable to the confusion and soul-searching IT managers faced as PCs stormed into their organization, or it may have been caused by increasing corporate discomfort about acquiring new information technologies with little regard to achieving a definable return on their investment.

Fortunately, about that time the cost of hardware and communications services began to decline very rapidly. This enabled IT to decentralize systems, fueled the PC revolution, and, perhaps most important, put computers on senior managers' desks.

Decentralizing information systems got senior managers and system users excited. However, this excitement faded as businesses faced increasing difficulty controlling and managing information that had been distributed from centralized mainframe computers to departmental servers and networked PCs. Many businesses wondered how they could ever integrate the mountains of disparate, incompatible hardware and software that they had acquired over the last ten years.

Difficulties in Controlling IT Costs
• It is very difficult to define users' requirements *before* a system is developed. Revising specifications *during* the development process increases costs.
• It is very difficult to estimate software development costs. Custom software projects are becoming more difficult to justify as user expectations grow.
• It is often necessary to scale hardware purchases to support anticipated system usage. Companies typically purchase more hardware capacity than necessary to accommodate future growth.
• Hardware and software become obsolete in two to three years. It is often impractical to maintain legacy systems because suppliers are unwilling or unable to support obsolete products.
• Senior management often takes a short-term view of IT requirements. IT managers face an uphill battle selling "infrastructure," such as upgrading network components. It is easier to justify more visible "productivity tools," such as notebook computers for outside sales representatives.

At this point, businesses began recruiting IT managers who focused on, or at least talked about, fast pay-back and quick turnaround to improve their businesses' competitiveness. However, while IT budgets continued to escalate, in many cases hard cost savings failed to materialize.

NETWORK COMPUTING CHANGES EVERYTHING

Over the last two years, as companies have begun to face the impact of global network computing, senior managers' concerns have shifted from competitiveness to survival.

There is no doubt that *network computing*—based on Internet protocols—has momentum. Businesses are making enormous investments in Internet and Intranet technologies to help ensure that they are able to maintain their market positions as businesses and consumers begin to conduct business on the Internet's World Wide Web.

As always, senior managements' rationale for deploying network computing technologies is based primarily on an intuition that their investment will position their companies to take advantage of the Internet, rather than on hard cost savings or predictable sales revenues based on their investment.

This "survival" mentality helps explain why many large corporations are investing millions of dollars to deploy commercial Internet sites, which they do not expect to be profitable for at least three to five years.

COMPETITIVE ADVANTAGE

While in principle aligning IT strategies with an organization's business strategies to achieve competitive advantage is a positive and reasonable objective, in practice it is very difficult to achieve.

The main reason for this is that an IT manager must balance the business's short-term objective of containing IT costs and providing reliable computing services, with its longer-term strategic objectives of improving competitiveness and ensuring that the organization survives the impact of emerging technologies.

The process of aligning IT strategy with business objectives has gone through four distinct phases:

- *1970's—Functional Systems*

    IT systems in each department automate specific functions.

    Priority: Implement functional systems

    Architecture: centralized, batch computing

- *1980's—Interoperable Systems*

    IT systems shared by multiple departments automate specific functions and share information.

    Priority: Automate the enterprise

    Architecture: decentralized, relational database models

- *Early 1990's—Reengineered Systems*

    IT systems across the enterprise are used to reengineer specific business processes to improve competitiveness.

    Priority: Improve competitiveness and contain costs

    Architecture: networked, interactive computing

- *Today—"Next-Generation" Systems*

    IT systems enable businesses to exploit opportunities that have resulted from technological innovation and "next-generation" network computing systems.

Network computing enables and/or compels businesses to re-value their business processes and output.

Priority: Survive impact of emerging technologies on fundamental business model

Architecture: network computing, support for Internet standards

IT STRATEGIES

From a short-term business perspective, an organization which has, for example, implemented a UNIX-based financial management system, a Macintosh-based desktop publishing system, and a Windows/NT-based Intranet server may have deployed the right systems at the time to meet its needs. But from a longer-term strategic perspective, the practical considerations which led to deploying these disparate systems may obviate the possibility of implementing a "next-generation" IT system, without replacing a great deal of the legacy IT infrastructure.

Replacing mission-critical legacy systems can consume an enormous amount of resources, and may put the organization at risk. PC-hosted relational database management systems (RDBMSs), for example, have failed to provide the data integrity and scalability of RDBMSs hosted on legacy mainframe computer systems. To preserve their investment in legacy RDBMSs, IT managers have been forced to implement complex three-tier client-server computing architectures and data warehousing strategies.

The less obvious reason that aligning IT strategies with an organization's business strategies is so challenging is that it is very difficult to articulate how an IT strategy *maps* to nebulous business objectives. Strategic IT decisions, such as whether to implement a Fast Ethernet or an ATM backbone, or whether to implement Lotus Notes or Microsoft's Internet Exchange Server, are difficult to map to a business's strategic objectives. They are usually justified by advocating politically correct advantages, such as "improving individual workers' ability to work together," or "improving management's ability to make timely decisions."

The truth is, information systems are extremely complex, and in most cases have been designed to support specific business needs, not to interoperate with legacy information systems, and not to address "strategic" business objectives. Industry insiders know that new products will *fail* to win market acceptance unless they have a clear message about what specific problem their technology addresses.

Interconnecting disparate systems using complicated networking applications and devices can re-define an organization's IT *architecture,* and can help it maintain mission-critical legacy systems which cannot, for reasons of cost or immature emerging technologies, be replaced with "next-generation" technology. But this does not define an IT *strategy,* and it does not directly address the organization's "strategic" concerns about improving competitiveness and ensuring survivability.

Aligning IT strategies to support your business objectives is a major challenge, but it can be achieved if you have a thorough understanding of your business objectives, legacy systems and emerging technologies.

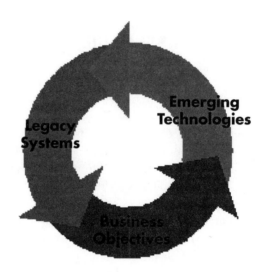

The information technology audit process is designed to help you achieve this understanding, and to enable you to balance your organization's two critical needs: to maintain cost-effective, mission-critical legacy applications, and to reposition itself for competitiveness and survival as emerging technologies impact your organization's fundamental business model.

BUSINESS OBJECTIVES

IT managers face a constellation of pressures to meet their business objectives:

- User demand to provide additional services, improve efficiency and increase effectiveness while containing costs.

- Competitive need to evaluate, integrate and deploy new technologies.

- Competition from internal "power" users, system consultants and integrators, and outsource suppliers, is making it increasingly difficult to justify increasing

IT budgets, because IT has lost its "monopoly" status as the sole provider of information services.

- Business managers are becoming aware that their value as an information company may already eclipse the value of the hard products or services that they manage; collecting, storing, analyzing, processing and disseminating information may in fact already be their primary business.

To overcome these concerns, IT must reengineer any practices, procedures, or attitudes that have become obsolete or irrelevant.

- *Obsolete Attitudes*—For example, the requirement for users to become "computer literate" has been simplified by graphical user interfaces and client-server computing. The Internet is a ubiquitous example of a system that is easy enough for "the rest of us" to use.

- *Obsolete Practices*—For example, inexpensive PC-based servers deliver better performance than proprietary minicomputer systems. It is no longer possible for most businesses to justify investing in obsolete minicomputer technology.

- *Obsolete Procedures*—For example, IT's role in custom application development has changed because new visual programming tools, such as Microsoft's Visual Basic, enable business users to develop their own applications and generate their own reports.

> The information technology audit process will help you identify the obsolete attitudes, practices and procedures that must be addressed before you can align your IT infrastructure with your strategic business objectives.

INFORMATION TECHNOLOGY CYCLES

IT has cycles, fashions and fads, like any other human endeavor. But to succeed, businesses must transcend these cycles to see clearly where, when and how emerging technologies can help them meet their objectives.

This is why it is imperative to implement an information technology audit; and this is why the audit process is such a valuable tool for defining an IT strategy that will help ensure your company's viability.

Yesterday's CIO	Today's CIO
• New technologies are good and should be implemented	• Cost containment is chief priority
• IT department is managed as independent "service" organization	• Focus on aligning IT services to meet core business objectives
• Develop new systems to stay ahead of competition	• Acquire "off-the-shelf" solutions to reduce costs and risks
• Build up internal skills and capabilities	• Outsource mission-critical applications to reduce costs and gain high-level IT management expertise
• Computers provide "data processing" services • Communication services are handled by the phone company	• Develop a comprehensive IT plan which includes a high-bandwidth communications infrastructure
• Automate tasks to streamline operations	• Develop a long-term (three- to ten-year) survival strategy using interoperable system components
• IT personnel have their own department—so we can focus on our core business	• The culture gap between technocrats and managers is putting the organization at risk
• Automate existing systems rather than consider new ways of doing business	• Use technology to reengineer and refocus the organization

MANAGING INFORMATION TECHNOLOGY

The primary purpose of an information technology audit is to help executive management understand and manage its information systems as a strategic business asset.

The information technology audit process is based on a step-by-step methodology that will enable you to analyze your unique business situation. The audit process begins by gathering information about your organization's business objectives, and about day-to-day operations. This will help you understand how and why specific systems have been implemented. You will be able to identify areas or tasks that can be made more efficient by upgrading existing systems or by implementing new technologies.

During the course of the audit, you will evaluate your organization's:

- Mission
- Objectives
- Operations
- Information technology systems
- Information technology department
- In-house development and user support
- Information systems security and reliability
- Information technology planning and management methodology

The following chapters contain over one hundred business audit and information technology audit worksheets that will provide a framework for your analysis. Specific examples of obsolete attitudes, practices, and procedures are identified in the sample worksheets.

After completing an audit, you should be able to prepare a report that includes:

- Evaluation of your information systems strategy.
- Evaluation of system implementation and security.
- Information on how emerging technologies, such as document management systems, "palmtop" computers and network computing can help your organization attain its business objectives.

IT AUDITS MUST BE TECHNOLOGY NEUTRAL

There is no "formula" for creating a successful IT infrastructure. Depending on your company's unique situation, there will be many factors that may make it more beneficial or cost effective to implement one technology rather than another.

Decisions about implementing new information systems should not be made before analyzing the pros and cons of implementing emerging technologies versus more established alternatives. For example, explore implementing next-generation network computing solutions before committing to more established client-server based solutions.

ARE YOU READY FOR AN IT AUDIT?

In most cases, one or more specific issues precipitates an audit. For example, your business might be concerned about an emerging technology, such as electronic commerce on the Internet; or you might be having difficulty managing your outside sales force; or questioning whether it makes sense to automate production scheduling.

WILL YOU NEED TO REENGINEER YOUR OPERATIONS?

Most organizations will be challenged to use their information technology audit results to change their business operations, and to automate tasks which are now being performed off-line. In some cases this will make sense; in other cases, solutions based on legacy technologies will provide a better balance between costs, benefits and risk.

In all cases, however, the audit process will enable your organization to have a clearer idea of what your business's needs are, and how the use of different technologies can help your organization develop an information technology infrastructure to support your strategic business objectives.

HOW LONG DOES THE IT AUDIT PROCESS TAKE?

Information technology audits generally take two to four weeks. If you become involved with extensive user requirements analysis, or longer-term strategic planning, it may take longer.

In any case, your organization should not implement any new technology unless it is confident that it can help increase revenues, decrease operating expenses, or provide obvious competitive advantage leading to new business opportunities. It takes time to gather enough information to make these decisions.

WHAT IS THE DIFFERENCE BETWEEN AN IT AUDIT AND REQUIREMENTS PLANNING?

The differences between an information technology audit and ongoing requirements planning involve objectivity, expertise, and window of opportunity.

- *Objectivity*—An information technology audit does not assume that automated solutions and new technologies can solve "every problem." An auditor is not responsible for the current state of affairs and doesn't have to defend it.

- *Expertise*—Most IT personnel are in an "operations management" mode. They do not have the time, or the knowledge base, to evaluate the impact of emerging technologies on their business operations.

  An auditor, by definition, must have the industry expertise to identify and understand the business implications of emerging technologies on a client's business model.

- *Window of Opportunity*—Most important, the information technology audit process provides an opportunity for businesses to step back and reevaluate their information systems, their support strategies and the potential impact of emerging technologies.

SELECTING AN AUDITOR

Information technology audits should be administered by an individual who understands computers and communication systems and is familiar with emerging technologies. In addition to possessing technical acumen, the auditor must be objective, have good analytical skills, and be able to focus on business issues without getting too involved in technical details.

In larger companies, the individual who manages the audit process may be the chief information officer, chief technology officer, vice president of information systems, or manager of the information systems department. In smaller companies, the auditor is often a business manager with limited computer technology skills, such as a PC "power user," who has the confidence of upper management.

As a rule, senior IT personnel are well equipped to perform a technology audit. However, lower-level IT managers and network system administrators are often too enamored with emerging technologies, defensive about their legacy systems, or out of touch with emerging technologies to be effective objective auditors.

If a qualified resource is not available within your organization, you should search elsewhere for a qualified consultant with a broad range of strategic planning and information systems experience. Any consultant you retain must demonstrate no conflicts of interest and no benefit from promoting any technology or supplier. Your consultant's only "agenda" should be your success.

MANAGING THE AUDIT PROCESS

An auditor's first priority is to understand the client's objectives for implementing an audit, and to reconcile any differences between the client's expectations and the services to be provided. The next step is to learn as much as possible about the factors the client believes are responsible for the success of the business.

In the process of gathering this information, the auditor will learn a great deal about how the business operates, and will have an opportunity to develop effective working relationships with the client's staff.

In this book, we will use the terms, "you," "auditor" and "consultant" interchangeably, depending on the context; and will sometimes refer to the audited business or organization as the auditor's "client." Auditors who are internal personnel can be more objective if they think of their own business as a "client" that has hired them to audit their IT systems.

The business audit worksheets in Chapter 4 will help you collect information from which you can analyze your client's success factors and business model. After reviewing these worksheets with your client, and verifying that they are accurate and complete, you will be ready to assess the effectiveness of your client's IT systems.

When you have completed the technology audit worksheets included in Chapter 4, you should review your findings with your client's IT personnel. By comparing your client's success factors with your worksheet results, you should be able to identify areas which could benefit from new or modified IT systems. At this point, you will be ready to evaluate emerging technologies, using the guidelines in Chapter 6, to determine whether specific technologies may be of strategic importance to your client.

After completing these two sets of worksheets, reviewing them with senior management, and surveying emerging technologies, you should be prepared to summarize your findings and recommendations in an information technology audit report.

In this you should describe any functional or operational problems that you have observed during the course of your analysis, present information on how specific technologies can be leveraged to help your client support operations, and summarize any recommendations that you have regarding emerging technologies.

Depending on your recommendations, it may be necessary for you to help your client "visualize" how specific technologies can help the business achieve particular objectives. For example, you may want to schedule mini-seminars or demonstrations, supervise pilot projects, or invite technology suppliers to make presentations or respond to one or more requests for proposal.

By implementing an information technology audit and having a strategy in place for monitoring emerging technologies, you can position your company as an early technology adopter and win competitive advantage over less technologically advanced competitors.

CHAPTER

2

THE IMPACT OF EMERGING TECHNOLOGIES

Information systems provide the cornerstone of today's business.

It is difficult to identify a segment of our economy that has not been impacted by emerging computer and communications technologies. In virtually every business, profitability and competitiveness depend on the successful, timely adoption of new computer and communication technologies to improve efficiency and profitability.

In the retail pizza business, for example, point-of-sale (POS) systems are used to enter orders, and to route instructions to the food preparation stations; "back office" computers are used to track inventory, sales and payroll; telephones, fax machines and electronic mail systems are used to communicate with customers; and remote communications applications are used to transmit sales, marketing and operations data to headquarters-based computers.

To identify the technologies which can provide the greatest reductions in your operating expenses, and to improve your own business's competitiveness, you must focus on the impact of emerging technologies on the core "value" that your business brings to your market.

COMPETITIVE ADVANTAGE

Emerging technologies such as cellular telephones, portable computers, and "palm-top" personal digital assistants can provide a competitive advantage to early technology adopters. However, you must balance the potential value of reducing the cost of doing business, improving customer satisfaction, and improving competitive position in new markets, with the risks inherent in adopting emerging, often unperfected technologies.

CELLULAR TELEPHONES

The cellular telephone is a good example of how an emerging technology can transform business operations. They are not perfect. Open channels are not always available, sound quality is not as good as land lines, and calls are occasionally dropped when transferred between different cellular carriers. Nonetheless, cellular telephones have effectively de-coupled business people from their desks.

When they first came to market, cellular telephones provided a competitive advantage for early technology adopters, such as outside salespeople. This window of opportunity lasted about twelve months. After this early-adopter phase, the cost of using a cellular phone dropped significantly; telephones were given away to customers for signing a one-year service contract, and the cost of per-minute access time fell to less than thirty cents. Today, millions of business people rely on them to provide better customer service, and to help them better manage their time.

PORTABLE COMPUTERS

Most business people today take portable computers for granted. Yet only a few years ago, they were two to three times as expensive, weighed twice as much as current models, could not operate for more than about an hour on a battery charge, and could not store enough information, or process applications fast enough, to replicate the user's desktop PC environment.

As technology improved, business people adopted portable "notebook" computers to help them access customer information, make sales presentations, communicate with their business partners, send and receive electronic mail, and access Internet Web sites around the world.

PERSONAL DIGITAL ASSISTANTS

Personal digital assistants (PDAs), or "palmtop computers," are another example of an emerging technology that, although constrained by technological limitations, is gaining market momentum by solving real world problems.

Although not as mature a technology as portable computers or cellular telephones, PDAs have integrated handwriting recognition software, infrared connectivity to peripherals, scaled-down versions of popular PC software packages, and modems to support telecommunications and remote data access.

These innovations have overcome many, but not all, of users' concerns about palmtop computing. It is, for example, difficult to get information into and out of a palmtop computer because there is no room for a normal-sized keyboard. Wireless, infrared keyboards are useful in the office, but don't provide a solution when a palmtop computer is carried away from the user's desk. And while handwriting recognition has improved significantly over the last ten years, it still requires printing (no cursive writing), patience and persistence to input data accurately.

Palmtop computers will be much more attractive to business users when they can understand human speech. However, voice recognition technology is not perfected yet. Voice recognition systems can only support limited vocabularies, and an individual's enunciation, timing and inflection all impact how well the software can recognize speech patterns of different individuals.

Although most business people feel that they can handle their personal organizational challenges more effectively with a paper-based time-log and address book than with a palmtop computer, early technology adopters are using PDAs to replace their pocket day planners. PDAs are also being used to support mission-critical data entry applications, such as filling out accident reports in the insurance industry and proof-of-delivery receipts in the transportation industry.

Number of Personal Digital Assistants Shipped
Source: The Yankee Group (Values for 1996 on are estimates)

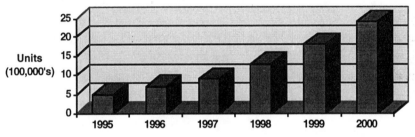

IMPACT ON YOUR BUSINESS MODEL

The examples of cellular telephones, notebook computers and personal digital assistants illustrate how emerging technologies can provide a window of opportunity for early technology adopters to gain a competitive advantage by implementing new products when they are mature enough to solve real business problems. Such an advantage can lead to rapid change in the marketplace. And these changes, precipitated by emerging technologies, can fundamentally alter an entire industry's business model. Retail travel agencies provide an outstanding example of how this happened.

Travel agencies serve their customers by providing travel information, and by acting as sales agents for travel-related products and services. Their revenues are derived almost entirely from commissions on the reservations that they book for travel suppliers.

In the past, United Airlines paid independent travel agencies a 10% commission on each domestic airline ticket issued. In 1995, it capped the commission for this service at $50.00. One reason it was able to do this was that it implemented electronic ticketing on many of its domestic flights. Electronic ticketing obviated the need to issue paper tickets, and eliminated some of the "value" that travel agencies used to justify their 10% commissions.

United Airlines' next step was to develop a software reservation application, called United Connections, which enables United's customers to use their own PCs to reserve flights, make hotel and car rental reservations, make credit card payments, and request special services, such as aisle seats, vegetarian meals, non-smoking rooms, and specific types of rental cars. Early technology adopters (PC-savvy business travelers) are using United Connections to help them save time, and have more control over their travel arrangements.

Travel agencies must respond to these emerging reservation "technologies," which have already impacted their fundamental business model, by providing additional value (travel-related services) to their customers. Otherwise, they will continue to lose market share as their customers move their business to online travel agencies that can provide equivalent services and in-depth travel information.

The take-home message for businesses today is that they must be proactive in identifying emerging technologies that may impact the value that they provide to their customers, employees and shareholders. Otherwise, they may discover that emerging technologies have redefined their fundamental business model, and that they can no longer compete effectively within their own market.

EVOLVING SYSTEMS
ARCHITECTURE

Five years ago, most business people thought of their computers as electronic file cabinets. Today, they think of them as "servers" or "appliances" which provide different services, such as information access and data communications.

The most important factor impacting both improvements in computer and communications technology and rapidly declining costs of data communications is the extraordinary advances in microcomputer design and manufacture over the last 35 years. The engineers and scientists responsible for developing these technologies are, in a sense, the "fathers" of our world's Information Age.

MICROPROCESSORS: SMALLER, FASTER, AND LESS EXPENSIVE

In 1965, Gordon Moore, who later founded Intel Corporation, predicted that the computing capacity of computer chips would double every year. Moore based his prediction on the fact that the price-to-performance ratio of computer chips had doubled every year for the previous three years. Ten years later Moore changed his prediction, to say that computational capacity would double every two years.

Computational capacity, as measured by a microprocessor's transistor count, has doubled about every 18 months over the last thirty years, and Moore's prediction has come to be known in the industry as Moore's Law.

Intel's 32-bit Pentium Pro processors, for example, have two to five times the computational capacity of Intel's last-generation Pentium processors; Intel's next-generation 64-bit microprocessors will have six to ten times as much computational capacity as today's Pentium Pro processors.

As more powerful microprocessors are incorporated into new computers, their price-to-performance ratio will improve dramatically. Business users will be able to afford to implement new applications, such as 3-D graphical user interfaces, video-conferencing, and new applications which have not yet been developed.

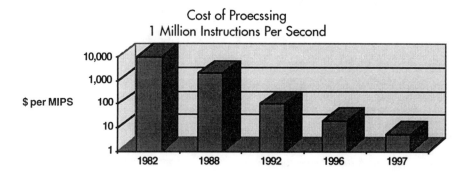

Cost of Proecssing
1 Million Instructions Per Second

DATA STORAGE

The cost of storing information is also declining rapidly. Both short-term memory chips and longer-term magnetic and optical storage devices are experiencing the same trends as microprocessors—they are becoming *faster, smaller,* and *less expensive.* Emerging data storage technologies such as magnetic/optical hybrid disk drives, and Digital Video Disk (DVD) drives will enable computer and communication systems to become even smaller, faster and less expensive than existing storage options. DVD disks, for example, can store over 7 gigabits of data, or over two and a half hours of full-motion compressed video with CD-ROM quality sound, on a disk the size of a standard CD-ROM. DVD drives can read standard CD-ROM disks, and are expected to obsolete CD-ROM drives over the next five years.

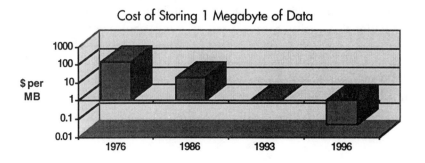

Cost of Storing 1 Megabyte of Data

PERIPHERALS

The cost of computer peripherals, such as printers, page scanners, and modems, is also declining, although at a slower rate than microprocessors and other semiconductor components. A Hewlett-Packard Laserjet printer, for example, which sold for about $6,000 in 1986, would sell today for less than $500.

Computer "ergonomics" are becoming more important to business users. Most businesses will, for example, pay a premium for the lightest-weight notebook PCs, 17" or larger color monitors, ergonomic keyboards and wireless pointing devices. And many businesses that cannot justify color laser printers are buying inexpensive color ink-jet printers instead of similarly priced black and white laser printers, because working with color monitors has raised their expectation for computer output.

SOFTWARE: FEATURES, INTEROPERABILITY, EASE-OF-USE

Software development is also moving at an extremely rapid pace. Today's software applications are providing increased functionality, improved interoperability and data sharing, and dramatically improved ease of use.

New software application development has become easier and faster thanks to new "visual" rapid application development (RAD) tools which enable programmers to select and link program components, called "objects," together. But while object-oriented application development has lowered the cost of new software applications, the cost of installing, implementing and maintaining software has not fallen over the last five years.

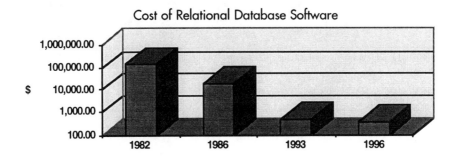

Cost of Relational Database Software

DOCUMENT RETRIEVAL SYSTEMS: A CASE STUDY

Declining hardware costs, advances in local area networking, and object-oriented development tools have enabled many businesses to reengineer their office systems by implementing document management systems. Page scanners, for example, which cost thousands of dollars a few years ago, are available today for less than one hundred dollars.

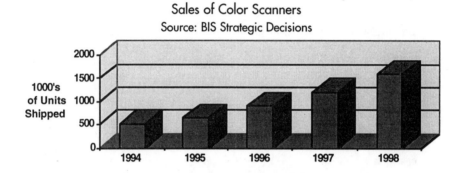

Businesses that could not justify the cost of deploying document management systems in the past can now implement this technology for several hundred dollars per workstation.

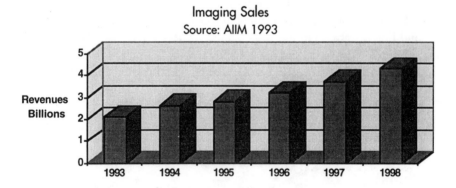

WHAT YOU SEE IS NOT ALWAYS WHAT YOU GET

Document management systems can lower the cost of doing business and provide competitive advantage. But implementing a DMS requires a great deal of expertise and an even greater amount of common sense.

Electronic Document Storage and Retrieval
1. Prepare Document
2. Append Bar Code—optional
3. Scan Document—convert image to digital representation.
4. Index Document—record index entries for document retrieval.
5. Store Document—can use computer output to laser disk technology and various data compression schemes.
6. Process Document—can automatically route document through an electronic mail system to different workstations.
7. Audit Process—make sure that the document is processed properly and verify that the scanned image is readable.
8. Data Security—make sure that document is secure from unauthorized access, and is protected with off-site backup.
9. Data Integrity—make sure that document is protected against unauthorized revision or edit, and that all document revisions are stored as needed.
10. Retrieve and View Document—provide connectivity from users' workstations to document storage media.
11. Reports—provide reports necessary to manage document storage and retrieval, evaluate user productivity, ensure security and data integrity, and support related business operations.

The DMS process appears at first glance to be very straightforward—connect up a scanner, make sure you have enough disk storage, buy software to manage the process and you're in business. Unfortunately, first glances can be very deceiving. Integrating the hardware to support a DMS and scanning and storing documents have become fairly simple. This is the easy part. But managing the process and integrating a DMS with other systems can be very difficult.

THE REAL WORLD

Implementing a DMS requires the system integrator to understand the user's requirements, database design methodologies, hardware, software integration issues, and workflow analysis. It is a complex business, and many "real world" problems can arise as IT wrestles with different aspects of the integration process. For example:

1. Documents that are stored electronically need to be retrieved using a search key, which serves as an electronic "pointer" to a specific document. It is important to select search keys that make it as easy and efficient as possible to locate stored documents.

   At first, it appears that using lots of search keys will solve this problem. But maintaining unnecessary search keys is a waste of time and money. Unless user requirements are well understood, the DMS system will be extremely cumbersome to use.

2. Information must be entered into the DMS index accurately. If the name Otto is, for example, indexed as "Otta," users will not be able to find Otto's documents using "Otto" as a search parameter.

   Many companies use bar codes to facilitate their indexing process. They can be scanned automatically, saving data entry time and eliminating many data-entry errors. But it is not always possible to attach bar codes to documents as they are created.

3. When a sheet feeder on a scanner accidentally pulls two documents through at one time, one is digitized and one is "lost." Users must implement an audit step to make sure that every document is scanned, and that each document has been scanned correctly so that each electronic image is legible.

Parallel Systems. If an automated system doesn't work properly, a manual system will be developed in parallel to enable the organization to get its work done. If a DMS doesn't work properly, the organization will need to maintain paper files. Unfortunately, running "backup" manual systems with automated systems is not uncommon. IT managers and senior managers often spend years justifying ineffective information systems in the mistaken belief that an incorrectly specified or implemented technology is going to improve their productivity.

> IT managers must balance the risks of implementing new systems, the advantages of adopting emerging technologies, and the very practical reality of their organization's need to maintain a reliable, cost effective information systems infrastructure that can meet their current and future needs.

EMERGING BREAKPOINTS

There are many technology breakpoints that can enable businesses to reduce their costs, improve their profitability and develop new business opportunities.

Emerging Breakpoints	
Processors	Intel Pentium Pro, P7 and P8 Motorola Power PC Digital Alpha Processor
Client	Microsoft Windows NT Netscape Browser Network Computer
Server	SMP Servers Microsoft Back Office Server Management Systems
Data Storage	RAID CD-R storage DVD Technology
Networking	(Private) Intranets (Public) Internet Lightweight Directory Access Protocol (subset of X.500)
Communications	ISDN, ADSL, ATM Virtual, Switched Networks Cable Modems
Remote / Wireless computing	Infrared (IrDA) Standard CDPD Communications Satellite Communications
Collaborative Computing	Lotus Notes - Internet Version Microsoft's Exchange Server Intel's ProShare Videoconferencing
Management	SNMP and RMON Desktop Management Initiative Novell Directory Services

1980: THE USER STRIKES BACK

In 1980, the computer industry experienced the PC Revolution. The PC Revolution empowered business people to automate many tedious office functions, such as creating and editing documents, and enabled businesses to move some of their mission-critical applications from a centralized computing model to a distributed computing model. The primary force behind this revolution was a desire by business users to have better access and control of the information they needed to achieve their business objectives.

There was, in addition, a hidden agenda behind the PC Revolution. It was the users' desire to gain independence from IT professionals who had distanced themselves by becoming data "librarians," who could only provide limited access to critical corporate information. The primary impact of this paradigm shift was to improve individual workers' ability to process information, and to move decision making from corporate headquarters to business managers in the field.

The major side effect of the PC Revolution was to propagate disparate systems throughout the organization. They became the nemesis of data management and cost containment, and were the undoing of conservative IT managers who continued to play the role of data "librarians."

Although most corporate information still remains on mainframe computers, the PC Revolution has been a success. Most mainframe computers now function as information servers in distributed information systems. And over 140 million "intelligent" PCs have subsumed the role of "dumb" mainframe computer terminals, and are being used in virtually every business, and in over 35% of all U.S. households.

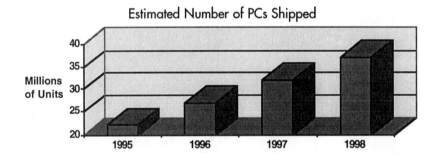

1985: LET'S GET CONNECTED

In 1985, the PC Revolution was eclipsed by the Local Area Network Revolution. Local Area Networks (LANs) comprised of PCs and shared network resources, such as laser printers and high capacity data storage units, enabled businesses to leverage their expanding investment in PC technology.

The LAN revolution was a welcome relief for most users, because it provided better access to corporate databases and enabled users to share information and electronic mail. However, it was no panacea for IT managers. Most IT managers spent the next five years resolving network management issues involving the same data security, data integrity and systems management problems that had plagued their centralized systems for the previous fifteen years.

Despite these problems, the LAN Revolution continues to gain momentum. According to a report by International Data Corporation published by Novell, Inc., over 100 million users were connected to networks in 1995. IDC estimates that over 200 million users will be LAN-enabled by the year 1999, and that over 125 million of those users will have electronic mail boxes and some level of Internet access.

NETWORKING TRENDS

About 80% of local area networks run on standard 10 Mbit/sec. Ethernet protocols. The other leading network protocol is Token Ring; which has been promoted by IBM.

Many companies are upgrading their Ethernet networks to support 100 M bit/sec. Fast Ethernet (100Base-T) protocols. Fast Ethernet provide better support for higher-bandwidth multimedia applications running on Pentium and Pentium Pro processors.

Many companies are also installing Switched Ethernet hubs which segment networks into subnets. Each switched subnet can use Ethernet's entire bandwidth to improve network performance. For example, a 100Base-T switched Fast Ethernet hub provides 100M bps bandwidth to the workstations (nodes) connected to each switched port. Many companies are implementing dual 10-100 Ethernet switches to help them migrate from Ethernet to Fast Ethernet hubs.

Higher bandwidth protocols such as ATM (Asynchronous Transfer Mode) which runs at up to 155M bps and 1G bps Ethernet are also being implemented by early technology adopters. These protocols have been optimized to support high-bandwidth multimedia and Internet applications. At this point, 1G bps Ethernet appears to have an advantage in the network protocol wars because it maintains backward compatibility with Ethernet and Fast Ethernet.

1990: THE CLIENT, THE SERVER, AND THE UNCONNECTED

In 1990, the computer industry began moving toward a client-server computing model. On the software side, client-server applications partitioned computing tasks between "client" applications running on networked PC computers, and "server" applications running on powerful application, database, communication and network servers. On the hardware side, microprocessor-based PCs and Symmetric Multiple Processor (SMP)-based PC servers containing multiple CPUs began replacing proprietary minicomputers and mainframe computers.

Digital Equipment Corporation, for example, has replaced most of its VAX mainframe computers with its Alpha microprocessor-based servers. It has also pioneered "clustering" technology which links multiple processors together to provide hot-standby failover, scalabilty, high availability, and a fail-safe file system—while appearing to users and system managers as one computer system, rather than a cluster of multiple systems.

CLIENT-SERVER AT WORK

Dividing processing between a *client* workstation and a "back-end," *server* application allows users to take advantage of powerful PC workstation's user-friendly presentation capabilities, and a high performance application server's file management and data processing capabilities.

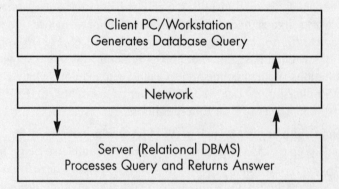

In addition to leveraging the computational power of PC workstations, client-server database applications reduce the amount of network traffic. This can dramatically improve system performance, because the only information that needs to be transmitted across the network is the client PC's requests for information, and the server's response; data files do not have to be loaded into the "client" workstation to be processed.

By using a standard database interface (API), such as Microsoft's ODBC, users can use the client application that is best suited to their particular task. For example, users might use a report writer, or a decision support tool such as Microsoft Excel to access their corporate information base.

REMOTE ACCESS COMPUTING

Client-server also provides an excellent platform for remote access computing which has evolved to support higher speed digital modem connections, and integrated POP or "point of presence" solutions comprised of remote access servers, routers and firewalls.[1]

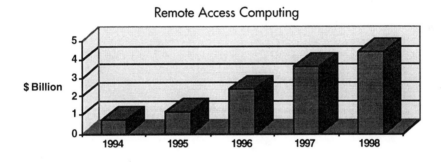

1995: "RECENTRALIZATION"

By 1995, IT managers were just beginning to understand how to implement and manage client-server applications. So of course, it was time for a "paradigm shift." Fortunately, 1995 was also the year Sun Computers, Netscape Communications, IBM, Oracle and over 100 other companies decided to give Microsoft and Intel (the "Wintel" Axis) a run for their money, by promoting a network computing architecture based on reengineering client-server applications into "component" software based on distributed business objects.

This assault would have been stillborn except for the simple fact that network computing provides a simpler, more efficient and ultimately more powerful computing infrastructure than LAN-based, client-server computing.

---

[1] A router is a device (computer hardware and network software) that is used to control the flow of information (route data packets) across a computer network. A firewall is a device used to monitor traffic between two computers to prevent unauthorized access to protected data.

The emerging network computing architecture is, in one sense, a return to centralized computing, with "thin" clients and powerful (host) servers. (Hence the moniker "recentralization.") But today's PC clients have more computational power than decade-old mainframe computers. And high data transmission rates through high-speed digital modems are making the *location* of data and data processing services transparent to system users.

NETWORK COMPUTING

Network computing enables users to "transparently" access programs and data stored on their own workstation, on their own Local Area Network, and on Internet "Web" servers which may be physically connected anywhere (literally around the world) on the Internet.

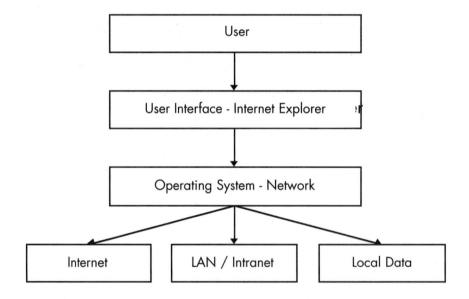

The Internet uses standard protocols based on HTTP, or Hyper Text Transfer Protocol. HTTP enables users to access information that is stored on different Internet servers by identifying the server's URL, or Universal Resource Locator address.

The Internet also uses a standard document format called HTML, or Hyper Text Markup Language, to "publish" information on Web "pages." An Internet (World Wide Web) browser can read any Web page that is stored in HTML format.

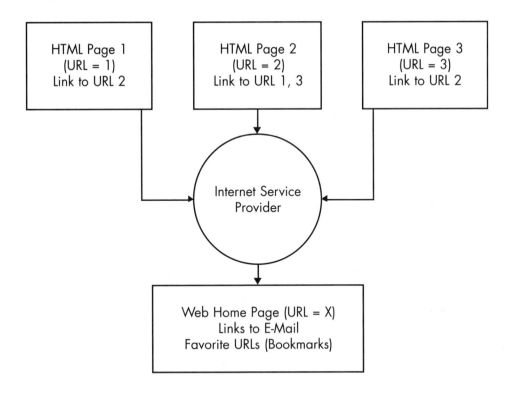

In the exhibit, the user's Web browser enables the user to connect from the Home Page on the Internet Service Provider's (ISP) Web server (URL=http:\\www.x.com) to any other Internet server. HTML pages 1, 2 and 3 are on different Web servers that are connected to the Internet. As indicated, the user's home page usually includes predefined links (bookmarks) to the user's favorite Web sites, and to a personal e-mail post office box.

It will probably take three to five years before network computing-based systems can provide the same level of data access, integrity, security, and manageability as distributed client-server computing does today. So it's not time to scrap your company's mainframe, or replace your recently implemented client-server applications. But it is time to begin thinking about the strategic implications of Internet applications developed using advanced component software architectures.[2]

---

[2] IDEA in Billerica MA forecasts that "By the year 2000, there will be more than 120 million installed Internet seats (users), more than 60 million installed Intranet seats, and more than 30,000 SNA hosts and 150,000 AS/400 hosts representing 4 million seats that could want Internet and/or Intranet access." Source: *Network World,* May 20, 1996.

OLAP Meets the Internet

As information systems scale up in size, it becomes more difficult to find and access data.

Organizations which have implemented mission-critical applications on mainframe computers, for example, often deploy data warehouses which contain subsets of their data on smaller scale computers. OLTP (Online Transactions Processing) detail files are maintained on the mainframe, and summary information is maintained in a high-performance RDBMS hosted on one or more fast application servers.

This data can be accessed using Online Analytic Processing (OLAP) tools and report writers to help managers analyze different "views" of their data to spot trends and potential problems, and to perform "what if?" data analysis.

In the early 1990's OLAP was promoted by database tool suppliers as the ultimate way to enable managers to access their corporate information stores, and to improve their decision making. The term "OLAP" has been integrated into the marketing stories of many database tool vendors, and it has become difficult to define exactly what it means. It originally referred to multidimensional analysis, but at this point, any database tool that does a cross-tab or supports drill down is claiming it supports OLAP.

Another new database term is "data mining." In its broadest definition, data mining refers to any tool which enables a user to analyze and understand data. However, a narrower and more useful definition is that it is a tool which employs a set of automated techniques to explore complex relationships in very large datasets.

To accomplish this, data mining tools explore numerous multidimensional data relationships concurrently, and use pattern-matching algorithms to identify key relationships. Data mining tools are proactive about finding data relationships, while OLAP tools support a verification-based approach, in which the user supplies a hypothesis about specific data relationships and then uses the tool to test their assumptions.

The Internet and network computing is having a tremendous impact on database access and data warehousing, because the goals of the Internet and OLAP (and data mining) tools are essentially the same: they help users find and access specific information stored in extremely large information bases. The Internet's TCP/IP and HTTP protocols provide an efficient mechanism to realize the benefits of client-server computing, provide a portable, easy-to-use client interface, and obviate a great deal of the complexity associated with remote data access.

Many organizations are already migrating to internal Intranets to help them access and manage their corporate information. In 1995, for example, more Web servers were sold for internal corporate Intranets than for external Internet use.

Many existing client-server applications and database tools have been adapted to work over Internet protocols, and a great deal of the research and development work that is being targeted at Internet-related problems will also help solve large-scale data management problems.

CONVERGENCE

Within 10 years, it will be possible to purchase a personal communication device that is roughly the size of today's portable cellular telephone. It will provide high-bandwidth, voice-enabled Internet access, entertainment on demand, and "personal assistant" functions such as daily planning and video recording.

This type of device will be a product of a phenomenon called "convergence," which refers to the merging of computing, communications and media (entertainment and information publishing) technologies. Emerging multimedia applications will become commonplace as it becomes less expensive to provide high bandwidth communications.

Emerging Multimedia Application	Bandwidth Required
• Telephone Quality Audio	64 Kbps
• Videoconferencing	128 Kbps to 1 Mbps
• MPEG Video	1.54 Mbps
• Imaging	8 Mbps to 100 Mbps
• Virtual Reality	>100 Mbps

THE INTERNET

Nicholas Negroponte, founding director of Massachusetts Institute of Technologies' Media Lab, states in his seminal work *Being Digital* that "Computing is not about computers anymore. It is about living. . . . As we interconnect ourselves, many of the values of a nation state will give way to those of both larger and smaller electronic communities. We will socialize in digital neighborhoods in which physical space will be irrelevant and time will play a different role."[3]

The infrastructure that we will use to "interconnect ourselves" is the Internet. Over 40 million people around the world are currently using it to communicate, conduct business, and entertain themselves. In the future, as problems of data integrity, security and high-bandwidth access are solved, hundreds of millions of people will access the Internet for both personal and business uses.

The Internet's primary use today is electronic messaging; however, many companies are using it to publish information, and to sell and support their products and services. As more commercial applications are developed and deployed, and as more compelling entertainment options such as video-on-demand become available, the Internet will become even more compelling to business users.

Businesses, such as publishers, whose products and services can be digitized and communicated electronically, have experienced the most profound impact on their business model. However, virtually every retailer, distributor, manufacturer and service organization that adds value by creating and distributing products or ideas will ultimately be impacted by the convergence between computers, communications and media.

INTERNET APPLICATIONS

- Worldwide electronic mail
- Mailing lists
- Information retrieval—file transfer (FTP)
- USENET news groups (electronic bulletin boards)
- Internet chat
- Voice communications
- Videoconferencing
- Digital marketing and sales
- Customer support services
- Electronic data interchange (EDI)
- Undiscovered future applications

INTERNET MOMENTUM

The U.S. government has recently passed new legislation that deregulates the telecommunications industry. This legislation is expected to lower telecommunication

---

[3] *Being Digital*, Nicholas Negroponte, Alfred Knopf, New York 1995.

and data communication costs as new competitors enter the market and struggle to win customers.

One consequence of this legislation will be to provide lower cost "bandwidth" which will promote rapid development and deployment of the Internet. As Internet technology becomes less expensive to deploy, and easier to use, it will evolve at an ever-increasing rate.[4]

BUMPS ON THE INFORMATION SUPERHIGHWAY

The Internet's extraordinary growth faces three major challenges. First, "bandwidth" will continue to be a problem until very reliable high-speed networks are in place to support resource-consuming multimedia applications. Second, competing networking and Internet application standards may derail universal access to the Internet's services. Third, it is extremely difficult to secure Internet applications.

In other words, the information and resources you need may be available somewhere on the Internet, but you may not be able to find them. If you are successful, you may have insufficient bandwidth to access them. And if you develop your own Internet Web site, you may need to implement a firewall to protect your system from computer hackers and competitors engaged in corporate espionage.

Several companies have developed Web search engines called "robots" or "spiders" to help users find information. However, the problem of locating Internet resources will not be completely solved until comprehensive standards for Internet access are adopted.

One of the key standards that needs to be defined involves network directory services. They provide a "naming service," comparable to a massive telephone directory, to help users locate information and resources. Unfortunately, several competing "standards" have already been deployed to support network directory services. If universal standards aren't adopted over the next two or three years, it will become increasingly difficult to manage Internet resources.

MARKET DEMAND DRIVES TECHNOLOGICAL INNOVATION

At this point, no one really knows how global network computing will change our world. As new Internet applications are developed, "Internauts" will try them out. The useful ones will survive; the less useful ones will be forgotten.

---

[4] Reed Hundt, Chairman of the FCC, has stated that "The information sector will be 1/6th of the US economy by 1997, . . . and that information processing will be the world's largest industry, with revenues of over $2 trillion by the year 2000." Source: *Computer Reseller News,* February 13, 1995.

But despite the enormity of this phenomenon, it *is* possible to anticipate the impact that the Internet, and other emerging technologies, will have on your business, because technological innovations are driven primarily by market demand.

For example, hundreds of companies are working on video compression and transmission, teleconferencing standards and consumer video products. It is safe to predict that within three years (an early technology adopter's "window of opportunity") new "desktop" videoconferencing products will emerge, and video mail on the Internet will eventually become as cost effective as e-mail and voice-only telephone communications are today.

If you believe that Internet applications, such as videoconferencing, will impact your fundamental business model, you should create an infrastructure within your organization to track this technology. And you should begin testing and adopting products which use these technologies as soon as they are mature enough to provide a competitive advantage to your organization.

THE YEAR 2000 PROBLEM

Moving into the year 2000 will be a problem for most companies, because many mission-critical applications assume that there is no year larger than 1999.

This is a serious problem, because many programmers over the last thirty years hard coded "19" into their programs, assuming that they would be replaced before moving into the 21st century. Their program's logic assumed a two-digit year for comparison and arithmetic. Since 00 is less than 99, these program's sort routines will no longer work properly, and the year 2000 will appear as 00 in reports and on inquiry screens.

If you do not have a year 2000 action plan, you should begin evaluating what steps your company will need to take to update your systems. This preparation will be the most labor-intensive data processing task ever faced, and many companies will procrastinate until they are unable to complete it on time.

FUTURE COMPUTING TRENDS

Each year technologies emerge that may enable your client to improve productivity, decrease expenses or capitalize on new business opportunities. The impact of these technologies on your client's business model can be anticipated to a great extent by tracking key trends in computer hardware, software, integration and support.

As we move into the 21st century, some of the most important technology trends will be to:

- Recentralize IT services (management, security, etc.).

- Outsource mission-critical IT services.

- Virtualize information access and processing using Internet protocols and network computing.

- Implement a component architecture built around business objects.

- Implement graphical interfaces everywhere.

- Adopt Windows/NT as the de facto standard client (PC) platform.

- Adopt Windows/NT Server as the primary standard for application and networking services.

- Use "visual" programming tools, such as Microsoft's Visual Basic and Sun's JAVA Script to enable users to customize their computing environment.

- Use Rapid Application Development tools such as Microsoft's Visual Programming tools and Borland's Delphi to speed corporate application development.

- Adopt scaleable SQL RDBMS for mission-critical applications.

- Deploy SMP and clustered servers to replace proprietary mini-computers.

- Face a "skills crunch" as IT personnel learn new technologies, such as object-oriented programming with Visual C++ and Java++.

FUTURE NETWORK TRENDS

Some of the most important network technology trends will be to:

- Migrate workgroup applications to individual users and departmental-level Intranet servers.

- Adopt TCP/IP (Internet) protocols (abandon Novell's IPX).

- Adopt HTTP (Internet) protocols for connectivity.

- Evaluate IIOP (Internet Inter-ORB Protocol) to deliver live, object-based components across the Internet.

- Adopt HTML (subset of SGML) for document portability.

- Migrate Local Area Networks from Ethernet, Token Ring, and other protocols to Fast Ethernet.

- Increase network bandwidth with switched Ethernet hubs to support users' demands for multimedia applications and Internet access.

- Adopt ATM and 1G bps. Ethernet to support high-speed data communications.

- Adopt ISDN today, and Digital Subscriber Line technologies over the next two to five years to support higher bandwidth Internet access.

- Adopt cable-modems in selected regions.

- Support electronic commerce and "digital marketing" on the Internet.

- Cope with global deregulation of telecommunications (money changes everything).

- Put in place wireless communications for Internet access.

- Establish remote communications for virtual / home office workers.

Networking Architecture	Typical Device or Application
Host / Server Operating System	AS-400 VMS
Network Operating System	UNIX Windows NT Server
Network Directory Services	Banyan VINES Novell Directory Services
Object Request Broker	CORBA, Distributed COM
Network Transport Protocol	Novell IPX TCP/IP
Backbone Protocol	FDDI ATM
Network Management System	SNMP / RMON Internet Management Tools

continued . . .

Networking Architecture	Typical Device or Application
Network Protocol	Ethernet / Fast Ethernet Token Ring
Bridges / Routers / Gateways	TCP/IP Internet Gateway Switched Ethernet Hub
Physical Layer	Category 3, 4, or 5 Fiber
Remote Connections	ISDN ADSL
Point-To-Point Connections	X.25 1 Gigabit Ethernet
Firewall	Backbone Level Application Level
UPS / Security	Automatic Notification Automatic Re-boot

Network Management Issues
• Automate hardware and software inventory
• Automate software distribution
• Automate software upgrades
• Ensure compliance with software licenses by monitoring and controlling application usage
• Monitor PCs to maximize availability
• Protect system by detecting and eradicating viruses
• Support help-desk operations
• Support disk backup
• Support workstation recovery ·

continued . . .

Network Management Issues
• Protect system from unauthorized access
• Enable system administrators to control network from a central console
• Set up custom procedures to run routine administrative tasks
• Simplify end-user interaction by customizing user interface
• Implement web-based management tools

FUTURE DATA MANAGEMENT TRENDS

Some of the most important technology trends in data management will be to:

- Migrate legacy DBMS applications to PC server-based RDBMSs to support client-server computing.

- Implement relational database management systems from leading suppliers (Oracle, Informix, Sybase, IBM and Microsoft).

- Implement client-server OLAP and data mining tools.

- Implement data warehouses and next-generation data marts (higher performance, subsets of data warehouses) and, to a lesser extent, operational data warehouses that support both data analysis and write access to source data files.

- Manage multiple (object-oriented) data formats, including text, unstructured multimedia, voice and video.

- Implement document management and imaging systems, and workflow applications to reengineer office procedures.

- Implement Internet-based database tools.

STRATEGIC BUSINESS AUDIT WORKSHEETS

The first phase of an information technology audit is to complete a strategic business audit.

The *strategic business audit* includes detailed worksheets that will help you define your business's objectives, position your products in your market, and analyze your business operations. It will also help you evaluate which areas of your business need to be reengineered to enable you to align your information systems with your objectives to increase profits, decrease expenses, and address new opportunities.

The worksheets can also identify areas of your business that may benefit from emerging technologies, such as network computing. You may complete a *strategic business audit* for your client, or have different worksheets filled in by the individual within your client's organization who is directly responsible for the specific area addressed by the worksheet. Your client's controller, for example, might complete those dealing with sales performance, budgeting, and accounting systems. Similarly, your client's DP manager might help you complete those on their MIS department.

In any case, the *strategic business audit* can be used to help you accomplish several objectives:

- Identify areas of your business that can be reengineered to improve productivity, decrease expenses, or enable your organization to enter new markets.

- Help you prepare a business plan.

- Help you reevaluate your fundamental business model.

- Help you evaluate merger and acquisition opportunities.

Depending on your audit objectives, specific worksheets may or may not be relevant. If you are working with an outside consultant, discuss your audit objectives to determine which worksheets are relevant to your audit before completing specific worksheets on your own.

AUDITOR'S NOTES

- *Visualize Your Own Situation*

  As you read through these sample worksheets, try to plug in your own business situation so that you can identify any obsolete attitudes, practices, and procedures that may impact your ability to align your IT systems with your business objectives.

- *Responsible Managers Should Complete Worksheets*

  Senior management should complete the worksheets on company effectiveness. Worksheets on individual departments or business units should be completed by their own managers.

- *Modify the Audit Worksheets to Meet Your Own Requirements*

  These worksheets are designed to provide an infrastructure to help you plan and implement your IT audit. However, you may need to modify some to reflect your own business.

IT AUDIT DISKETTE

Blank copies of every worksheet and sample form in this book are on the diskette that is included with this book in Microsoft Word (.DOC) format.

There are three files on the disk:

- BUSINESS.DOC (Contains blank copies of all business audit worksheets in .DOC format.)

- TECHNOLOGY.DOC (Contains blank copies of all technology audit worksheets in .DOC format.)

- CONSLT.DOC (Contains a copy of the consulting and independent contractor agreements in .DOC format.)

The information on the IT Audit disk is copyrighted and is licensed to the purchaser of this book pursuant to the terms printed on the disk's packaging.

EXAMPLE COMPANY: CLIENT-CENTERED™ TRAINING, INC.

Throughout this book, we have used a fictionalized version of Client-Centered™ Training, Inc., the author's training company, to illustrate the information technology audit process. Each worksheet has been "filled in" to provide an example of the depth of response required to complete a thorough audit. All references to individuals and businesses are fictional and are not intended to represent any real individuals or existing businesses.

As you read through this chapter, think about how you can use these worksheets to identify the obsolete attitudes, practices, and procedures in your own organization that you must consider before you can align your IT infrastructure with your strategic business objectives.

STRATEGIC BUSINESS AUDIT OBJECTIVES

As with any business activity, it is important to define your objectives before beginning a strategic business audit.

Key Objectives for Commissioning This Audit
Objective 1
Evaluate our current IT infrastructure to determine whether or not it is consistent with our business objectives.
Objective 2
Evaluate whether or not our IT budget is in line with other businesses in our industry.   *Determine where we may achieve cost savings without reducing our current service level.*
Objective 3
Evaluate whether or not it is advantageous to outsource our billing and receivables applications.
Objective 4
Evaluate our senior IT personnel's skills.
Objective 5
Evaluate the impact of the Internet on our business model.   *Evaluate the feasibility of using the Internet to help us market our services and support our customers.*

Most clients have three or four primary issues or concerns which have precipitated the IT audit. However, many clients have difficulty articulating all of their audit objectives. Spend as much time as necessary with your client to identify concerns and objectives before completing your audit worksheets. If you don't understand your client's objectives, you will not know which business areas to focus on.

GENERAL OBJECTIVES

The first three documents to prepare are a general information form, a company mission statement, and a corporate history. These represent basic pieces of information all companies should have readily available.

General Information
Principal Auditor: I.T. Master ("I.T.")
Date of Audit: 4/21/199X
Client Business / Organization: Client-Centered™ Training, Inc.
Address: 123 Bellevue Way, Suite 101, Bellevue, Washington
Client Contact: Doug Dayton
Phone: (206) 555-1212
FAX: (206) 555-1212
E-mail Address: DougDayton@ MSN.COM
Internet Web Site: WWW.C-CT.COM
Company / Organization's Founders: Doug Dayton and Terry Smith
Special Interests or Background: Doug Dayton and Terry Smith met at the University of Washington in 1976. Doug was interested in technology and education, and Terry was interested in law and administration. In 1985 they formed a training company to leverage their experience and education.

Mission Statement

Organization's Mission Statement

Client-Centered™ Training, Inc. helps technology-driven companies increase their sales by providing marketing and technical communications consulting and Client-Centered™ Training Seminars.

What product(s) does your business manufacture or resell?

- Client-Centered™ Training Seminars
- Client-Centered™ Training Guides and Books
- "Emerging Technologies for Decision Makers" Newsletter

What service(s) does your business provide or resell?

- Marketing and Technical Communications Consulting

Do you support or supply multiple distribution channels?

Yes, we sell books direct, and through our distributor.

We work with outside consultants who receive commissions for referrals.

Does your business sell your services the same way it sells its products?

No. We sell seminar programs and consulting services direct to our major accounts.

We do direct mail and telemarketing.

We sell our publications through book distributors and resellers.

We are exploring marketing on the Internet.

Does your business finance your product sales?

We provide 30-90 day terms to customers in good standing.

We work with a finance company to help us handle our larger customer's requirements.

We used to factor some of our receivables to help us manage cash flow during slow periods. We do not do this anymore.

Asking your client how its company was formed often provides useful insight into corporate objectives.

Corporate History
How was your company formed? Client-Centered Training was formed when several of our consulting clients asked us to develop custom training programs for their marketing personnel. We decided to "productize" our seminars and resell them to new clients.
Describe your corporate organization: (Sole Proprietorship / Partnership / Limited Liability Corporation / Corporation / S Corporation / Joint Venture / Public Corporation / Other) We are organized as a privately held corporation in Washington state.
What significant changes have occurred in your company's purpose and/or product focus since founding? Originally we developed application specific training courseware. However, we soon realized that there was a greater need in our market niche to provide executive level technology briefings and seminars on "emerging" technologies.
Are any ownership changes planned? We plan to issue key employees stock next year, and would like to do an IPO in two years when our sales reach $10 million. Are any Mergers or Acquisitions planned? We plan to acquire the rights to Dayton Associates' courseware. We want to use Dayton Associates' courseware as a basis for a new line of books on Strategic Business Planning.

Once you understand your client's most significant accomplishments and how, when and where your client provides value to their customers, you can begin identifying new business opportunities that leverage your existing business relationships.

Area of Company	Most Significant Accomplishments
Personnel / Organization	Our most significant organizational achievement was building a network of freelance consultants that we can utilize on projects which are too big for us to handle ourselves.
Product	Our new "Information Technology Audit Workbook on a CD" enables us to bring our IT Audit methodology to a much larger audience, and to provide this information at an extremely competitive price.
Service	Our Training Follow-Up Help Line provides faster response, has lowered our after-seminar support costs by over 15%, and helps us stay in touch with our customers' evolving training requirements.
Sales / Marketing / Distribution	We are considering implementing an Internet Web site to help us generate international sales.
Finance	We have secured a line of credit with the Big Bucks Bank. We have also engaged the Don't-Go-Way Credit Company to provide financing for our key accounts.
Technology	We have installed switched Fast Ethernet hubs and installed an ATM backbone. Our Internet server has a T1 connection to our Internet Service Provider.
Public Service	We have recently donated over $25,000 of our surplus office equipment to the Teen Success Program.

YOUR ORGANIZATION'S VALUE EQUATION

Corporations must provide value to their customers, employees and shareholders. If a corporation does not provide a reasonable return on shareholders' investment, its executive management will be held accountable. If it provides low employee wages or its benefits are not competitive with other employers in the market, it will suffer high employee turnover. And if its customers are dissatisfied, it will suffer declining market share.

When a corporation has created a balance between customer needs, employee demands, and shareholder expectations, its "Value Equation" is in balance.

VALUE EQUATION

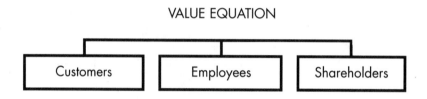

The primary objective of executive management is to maintain the viability of their organization by maintaining a balance between customer needs, employee demands and shareholder expectations. As a company becomes established and grows, its "value equation" will change. For example, a startup manufacturing company may provide its customers with a small number of products; as it grows, it may provide a better service level by supplying many more products that its customers need. Similarly, a startup manufacturing company may provide its production employees with at-will employment, while a more mature unionized shop may provide greater job security for senior staff.

What Value Does Your Business Provide?

Customers:

- We provide the highest quality training available.
- We provide custom programs with fast turnaround.
- We provide books and training guides to support our programs.
- Our consultants and trainers have extensive industry experience.

continued . . .

What Value Does Your Business Provide?

Employees:

- Dynamic, interesting workplace.
- Freedom to be creative and achieve recognition for contributions.
- Top 25% of industry compensation.
- Opportunity to advance with rapidly growing company.

Shareholders:

- Our sales revenues have grown 35% every year since our company was founded.
- Our corporate profits are being retained to finance growth.
- We anticipate having an IPO in two years.
- Our principals are very satisfied with their ROI.

Is your VALUE EQUATION in balance?

Yes. If we can maintain our profit margins and meet our revenue forecasts, our Value Equation will remain in balance.

BUSINESS OBJECTIVES

The next step is to identify the business objectives—both short and long-term—for the company. The worksheets are specific to the the particular time frame.

Short-term Business Objectives	Time Frame: Next Six Months
Profit	Increase 8%
Markets	Open Europe
Products or Services	Launch Client-Centered Selling
Production	Improve production turnaround

continued . . .

Short-term Business Objectives	Time Frame: Next Six Months
Sales / Distribution	Evaluate Asian distributors
Training / Support	Train sales force
Research and Development	Evaluate Dayton Associates materials
Financial (IPO etc.)	Interview investment bankers
New Businesses	Roll-out new advertising campaign in Southeast region
Company Involvement	Support Success Program
Other	

Longer-term Business Objectives	Time Frame: 6 to 12 Months
Profit	Increase profit by 20%
Markets	Open Asian market
Products or Services	Launch "Tracking Emerging Technology" Program
Production	Lease two new color laser printers
Sales / Distribution	Reestablish Southeast territory
Training / Support	Schedule "The Zen of Paying Attention" leadership program
Research and Development	Develop courseware based on Dayton Associates materials
Financial (IPO etc.)	Schedule outside financial audit
New Businesses	Work with European distributor
Company Involvement	Sponsor Success Program's annual fund raiser
Other	

ATTITUDES, PRACTICES, AND PROCEDURES

Client-Centered™ Training has made an effort to develop long-term business plans. However, most small companies and many mid-sized companies do not take the time to do this plann

Longer-term Business Objectives	Time Frame: One to Two Years
Profit	Maintain 20% after tax profitability
Markets	Grow international sales
Products or Services	Launch at least one program each quarter
Production	Bring seminar guide production in-house
Sales / Distribution	Schedule U.S. sales conference in St. Martin
Training / Support	Schedule all employees for "The Zen of Paying Attention"
Research and Development	Produce courseware based on Dayton Associates materials
Financial (IPO etc.)	Prepare for IPO
New Businesses	Acquire a multimedia production company
Company Involvement	Continue to sponsor the Success Program
Other	

Longer-term Business Objectives	Time Frame: Two to Five Years
Profit	Maintain 20% after tax profitability
Markets	Grow international sales - focus on Asia and Western Europe
Products or Services	Launch at least one new program each quarter

continued . . .

Longer-term Business Objectives	Time Frame: Two to Five Years
Production	Bring all seminar guide production in-house Publish 4 books each year
Sales / Distribution	Schedule first international sales conference in Venice
Training / Support	Select VP for Customer Service Department
Research and Development	Internationalize courseware based on Dayton Associates materials
Financial (IPO etc.)	Prepare for IPO
New Businesses	Acquire a multimedia production company
Company Involvement	Sponsor the success program and United Way
Other	

Longer-term Business Objectives	Time Frame: Five to Ten Years
Profit	Maintain 20% after tax profitability
Markets	Diversify into additional markets by localizing programs using native translators
Products or Services	Launch two training programs each quarter Publish 10 books each year
Production	Bring multimedia production in-house
Sales / Distribution	Move all products to internal Internet server
Training / Support	Develop a Train-the-Trainer program for Client-Centered Selling Seminar

continued . . .

Longer-term Business Objectives	Time Frame: Five to Ten Years
Research and Development	Schedule first yearly Personal Growth retreat
Financial (IPO etc.)	Consider merger and acquisition opportunities
New Businesses	Acquire additional multimedia production companies
Company Involvement	Sponsor the Success Program and United Way

MANAGEMENT OBJECTIVES

Every manager in your client's organization should complete an objectives worksheet. The two sample worksheets reflect the different objectives that the CEO and the VP of Sales have in our fictional company.

Manager: CEO	Objectives
Profit	Increase profits 20% Increase user base by 12%
Markets	Open European and Asian markets Identify distributor in South America
Products or Services	Develop one new IT program each quarter Improve telemarketing wait time
Production	Bring DVD production in-house Reduce training guide backlog to three weeks Decrease cost of materials by 10% and decrease waste by 15%

continued . . .

Manager: CEO	**Objectives**
Sales / Distribution	Increase sales by 18% Decrease travel expenses by 5%
Training / Support	Define training budgets and corporate policies for all employee training programs
Research and Development	Hire at least four more outside subcontractors Integrate Dayton Associates seminar materials into our existing courseware
Financial (IPO etc.)	Increase line of credit with the Go-For-Broke Bank Start meeting with investment bankers
New Businesses	Establish at least 15 new accounts this quarter
Company Involvement	Participate in all quarterly department reviews Write "from the top" article for our corporate newsletter

ATTITUDES, PRACTICES, AND PROCEDURES

Client-Centered™ Training could use the Internet to support low-cost international communications as it develops business relationships in Europe, South America, and Asia.

Manager: VP Sales	**Objectives**
Profit	Increase profit margins by 3% Increase profits on sales by 20%
Markets	Review territories in Southeast region Send Regional Manager to open Europe market Begin search for distributor in Asia

continued . . .

Manager: VP Sales	Objectives
Products or Services	Launch Client-Centered Selling training seminar Complete production of Client-Centered Selling training guide
Production	Coordinate sales forecast with production department to help reduce production delays
Sales / Distribution	Finalize contract with German production firm Review telemarketing scripts
Training / Support	Send all area representatives to time management seminar Have every telemarketer trained on new contact management program
Research and Development	Send new product requests and concerns to Development Manager
Financial (IPO etc.)	Enforce credit checking policy Require management sign-off on all seminar orders taken without 50% pre-payment
New Businesses	Evaluate sales potential of Dayton Associates training materials Submit findings at Manager's meeting
Company Involvement	

ATTITUDES, PRACTICES, AND PROCEDURES

Client-Centered™ Training may need to upgrade its networks to support demanding multimedia applications.

As you complete each worksheet, take time to think about any attitudes, practices or procedures that may affect your client's ability to align its IT systems with its business objectives.

CORPORATE CULTURE

Corporate culture plays an important role in the development of the organization.

Corporate Culture
Describe your corporate culture: For example: Chain of Command, Union Shop, Office of the Future, Professional Management Company, Work Teams, and so on.   • We believe in as little "top-down" management as possible. We empower our employees to take the initiative and make decisions. We recruit experienced professionals and expect them to take pride in their work.   • Since a great deal of our work is done by sub-contractors, we rely heavily on electronic mail to keep us focused and flexible.   • We don't wear suits, except on customer calls, and we try to maintain an informal "collegial" atmosphere.
How would you like your customers to perceive your company?   For example: "Leading Edge", Customer Oriented, Strong Product Focus, Service First, Value Leader and so on.   • We charge more for our services than some of our competitors. However, our customers demand a very high level of performance.   • We strive to meet our customer's expectations for professionalism and "style" in all of our communications.   • We want our customers to be surprised by the level of interest and concern we have in their success.

ATTITUDES, PRACTICES, AND PROCEDURES

Client-Centered™ Training's "humanistic" attitude toward its employees may signal a lack of concern about IT security.

PERSONNEL

Your personnel are your company's most important asset. Their strengths and weaknesses are your company's strengths and weaknesses. Learning how to cultivate their skills is key to building successful work teams.

Personnel	*Attach Organization Chart
Number of employees	18 (including contractors)
How many employees have left your company in the last year?	2
Do you periodically review your employees' performance?	Yes
What do you cover in employee reviews?	Objectives, key results, overall performance and compensation
Do you keep signed employee reviews and/or evaluations on file?	Yes
Do you feel your company is a fair, good, or great place to work?	Great
Do you publish an Employee/Company Policy Manual?	We have an employee manual that was created using a PC-based HR program. We plan to have our counsel review and update it next year.

ATTITUDES, PRACTICES, AND PROCEDURES

Client-Centered™ Training's use of a human resources software package indicates its comfort level with automating management processes.

ORGANIZATION CHART

- Attach an organization chart if one is available.

The organization chart is invaluable in helping you "visualize" how and where information systems can be implemented to support operations.

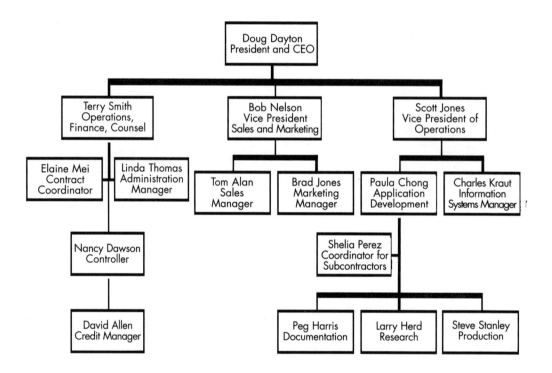

ATTITUDES, PRACTICES, AND PROCEDURES

Client-Centered™ Training could implement a collaborative conferencing application on an Internet server to help Shelia Perez manage relationships with C-CT's outside subcontractors. If C-CT implements an Internet server, it should consider using a firewall to prevent unauthorized access to its internal LAN.

Key Employees	Position	Salary	Shares, Options % Ownership
Doug Dayton	President	100,000	78
Terry Smith	Admin.	68,000	5
Robert Nelson	Sales	132,000	8
Scott Jones	Operations	81,000	5
Paula Chong	Development	72,000	2
Sheila Perez	Consultants	53,000	2

PLANNING ISSUES

The next worksheet concerns planning issues. Well-designed planning and reporting systems provide the "infrastructive" for effective business decision making.

Planning Issues	Status
Do you set goals [management by objectives] for your employees?	Yes - on a quarterly basis
Frequency of one-on-one meetings	Managers meet with direct reports every week
Frequency of departmental meetings	We meet every two weeks
Frequency of company meetings	We meet once every four to six months
Do you have appropriate non-disclosure, confidentiality and non-compete agreements on file?	No, but legal is working on this
Do you have key manager insurance policies in place?	Only for CEO
Do you have written job descriptions?	Yes
Do you have adequate incentives in place for key personnel? Are these reviewed periodically?	We are having a consultant review our compensation plan for hourly employees
Are your employee benefits competitive within your market segment?	Yes - we provide full medical coverage for employee's family
Do you maintain a Personnel Handbook that details company policies and employee benefits?	Yes, but it needs to be revised
Is your company unionized?	No
Do you increase employee participation through newsletters, staff meetings, after-hours social activities or other activities?	We have a corporate newsletter, but it is targeted at customers We have a TGIF party once a month at a local restaurant

continued . . .

Planning Issues	Status
Do you have company meetings and outings to help increase employee goodwill?	We have a summer softball tournament each year
Do you have an employee suggestion box? Do you provide incentives for suggestions that lead to reducing costs, improving products, or new marketing opportunities?	We don't have a suggestion box - but everyone has the president's e-mail address. We occasionally award bonuses for work that is above and beyond the call of duty
Would you rate employee morale as poor, good, or excellent?	Morale is very good
Are any personnel in your organization "irreplaceable?" List irreplaceable personnel	We are a small company - losing any of our senior managers would be a setback
Do you have a succession plan for these personnel?	We have department managers in Sales, Finance and Development that could be promoted. Our Operations department is weak.
Do you have a Board of Directors? If so, how often does it meet?	Yes - meets biannually
Include resumes for your Directors (optional)	To be attached
What additional expertise would be helpful on the Board?	We would like an IT expert on our Board to help us evaluate emerging technologies and to help us focus our IT strategy

continued . . .

Planning Issues	Status
Are any outside management consultants, analysts or advisors currently employed by your company?	We have retained outside counsel to review HR policies We are using a local system integrator to help us implement an Intranet server We work with an outside marketing company to create promotions We are using a trade show consultant

ATTITUDES, PRACTICES, AND PROCEDURES

Client-Centered™ Training could automate many of its processes using an electronic forms routing application. Once it is in place, C-CT could use it to help support future planning activities.

CORPORATE EFFECTIVENESS

The corporate effectiveness worksheets rate existing levels within the company on a scale of 1 (ineffective) to 5 (very effective).

Corporate Effectiveness—Part 1	1 (ineffective) to 5 (very effective)
• Market Share	2
• Price	3
• Margin	4
• Sales	3
• Profits	4
• Warranty	5
• Credit Terms	4

continued . . .

Corporate Effectiveness—Part 1	1 (ineffective) to 5 (very effective)
• Leasing	4
• Service	5
• Customer Training	3
• Inventory Control	4
• Aggressiveness Last Year	3
• Aggressiveness Today	3
• Reputation	4
• Customer Follow-up	3
• Other	

Corporate Effectiveness—Part 2	1 (ineffective) to 5 (very effective)
• Corporate Image	5
• Sales Management	4
• Financial Management	4
• Administration Management	3
• Employee Satisfaction	4
• Internal Training	4
• Day-to-day Operations	3
• Purchasing	3
• Financial Controls	4
• Inventory Control	2
• Manufacturing Efficiency	2
• New Product Development	2
• New Market Development	2

continued . . .

Corporate Effectiveness—Part 2	1 (ineffective) to 5 (very effective)
• Marketing	3
• Promotion / Advertising	3
• Executive Management / Board of Directors	4
• Other	

Department Analysis	Work Load	Job Skills
• Administrative	80% of capacity	Adequate
• Marketing	60% of capacity	Adequate
• Sales	85% of capacity	Senior
• Support	40% of capacity	Marginal
• Financial	70% of capacity	Adequate
• Production	105% of capacity	Adequate
• Research & Development	50% of capacity	Senior
• Manufacturing		
• Printing		
• Other		
• Other		

Note: Use one form for each department or workgroup.

Worksheets on department or workgroup level performance should be completed by a senior manager and by the relevant department or business unit manager.

Department Limitations	Function	Priorities
Administrative	No limitations	
Marketing	Advertising Telemarketing Direct Mail	Recruit three Telemarketing Representatives
Sales	International Sales	Locate distribution and marketing partners for Europe, South America and Asia
Support	Telephone Support	Link telephone support with Internet server database
Financial	Credit Line	Explore relationship with Big National Bank
Production	Packaging	Develop RFP for new packaging for new "In-The-Box" Training Programs
Research & Development	New Program Development	Hire outside consultant to facilitate a New Products Focus Session

MANAGEMENT EFFECTIVENESS

The management effectiveness worksheets rate a company's existing levels on a scale of 1 (needs improvement) to 5 (job well done). Individual department managers should complete their own worksheets.

Management Effectiveness	1 (needs improvement) to 5 (job well done)
• Leadership	4
• Vision	3
• Operations	2
• Corporate Marketing	3
• Delegation	5
• Organization	5
• Planning	3
• Motivation	4
• Finance	4
• Personnel	4
• Goal Setting	5
• Meeting Financial Goals	4
• Meeting Other Goals	2

Management Team's Effectiveness

What are the key strengths of your management team?

- *Our management team is excellent at communicating openly with no pulled punches.*

- *Each senior manager has over 10 years of experience in his or her field.*

continued . . .

Management Team's Effectiveness
• We have recruited overqualified managers so that they do not need to be replaced as our company grows.   • We have a good sense of our market, and stay focused on accomplishing our strategic objectives.
What are the key weaknesses of your management team?   • Our management team has not been successful at building efficient office systems. We waste time searching for information that should be available "on-line."   • We tend to be too patient with missed deadlines, and too humanistic when it comes time to let go an employee who is not performing up to our expectations.   • We have not been effective at developing new products, and have had to rely on our customers to help us stay abreast of the latest industry developments.   • We have not been effective at leveraging new technologies like the Internet.

Note: Use one form for each manager who has other managers as reports or who has P&L responsibility.

Individual Department Evaluation Production Department	**1 (don't agree)** **5 (strongly agree)**
Successful	3
Stable	4
Conservative	3
Formal	2
Organized	4
Autocratic	1
Aggressive	4
Creative	4
Opportunistic	3

continued . . .

Individual Department Evaluation *Production Department*	1 (don't agree) 5 (strongly agree)
Value leader	2
Service oriented	5
Profit oriented	5
Highly automated	4
Efficient	3
Bureaucratic	2
Other	--

Note: Use one form for each department.

FACILITIES

Most companies are located where they are because their founders lived there when they founded the company. Most do not consider relocation until growth pushes them into new, geographically distant markets.

There are many reasons why a company is in a specific location:

- Proximity to customers
- Proximity to suppliers and businesses in the same industry
- Tax base for community / state / nation
- Government subsidies / tax benefits
- Access to skilled employee pool
- Attractive local labor rates
- Access to educational institutions
- Access to government agencies
- Access to air, rail, land, and sea transportation
- Special business zoning
- Environmental considerations
- Political stability

- Cultural considerations and amenities

- Founder's / management's preference

Depending on the situation, one or more of these may be a "deciding" factor. For example, political stability is not usually a major consideration, until a business considers moving into an area that lacks it.

Type of Facility (Production Sales, etc.)	Location (Date Opened)	Satisfaction Level (Last Audit)	Current Status (Problems)
Headquarters	May, 1985	Acceptable	Re-design LAN Need new phone system
East Coast Sales Office	1994	Excellent	Need T1 link to main office, and Intranet server
West Coast Sales Office	1994	Excellent	Need T1 link to main office, and Intranet server
Production Facility	1995	Needs minor renovation in office area	Need color laser printer Need more space
When was the last time you performed a facilities audit?	Last year June, 1996		
Facilities Auditor:	Controller		

ATTITUDES, PRACTICES, AND PROCEDURES

Many fast-growing companies maintain their existing telephone equipment long after it should be replaced. C-CT may be able to install a PC-based telephone system to help it improve customer service.

Emerging standards, such as Microsoft's Telephone API (TAPI), are enabling computer telephony products to achieve a higher level of interoperability.

Expansion Plans	Next 6 Months	Next 24 Months	Next 36 Months
Manufacturing Facilities		Locate new production facility in London	
Service Facilities	Lease additional space		
Distribution Facilities		Find additional warehouse space	
Sales and Marketing Facilities		Open office in London	Open offices in Japan and Thailand
Administration Facilities	Remodel administrative offices		
Research and Development Facilities	Remodel room for network servers		
Other Facilities (Printing)		Locate printing equipment in production facilities	
Have you considered relocating any of your facilities to a foreign country to increase your company's competitiveness and improve your profitability?	See above		
Do you have any other expansion plans?	No		

FINANCIAL INFORMATION

This section contains financial information worksheets. Effective financial management depends on timely, accurate business reporting. Systems must be in place to analyze an organization's cash flow, projected cash requirements, and current business status.

Finance Department	Personnel
Chief Financial Officer	Terry Smith
Controller	Nancy Dawson
Treasurer	Terry Smith
Bookkeeper	Sandy Stone
Accounts Payable Clerk	Tracy Torino
Accounts Receivable Clerk	Anita Barnes
Administration Manager	Linda Thomas
In-house Legal Counsel	Terry Smith
Retained Legal Counsel	Peabody & Sherman
Outside Auditor / CPA Firm	Jones & Smith
Do you employ HR Counsel?	Yes
Do you have adequate insurance to cover your business, including errors and omissions, fire, theft and other potential hazards?	Yes
Have you had an insurance audit in the last twelve months?	No

Financial Information
Attach current and past three years financial statements and business plans.
Attach additional financial reports for the current year which describe your financial condition. *(To Be Attached Here)*

continued . . .

Financial Information
Cash flow analysis A/R Report A/P Report Inventory Report Sales / Bookings Report
Does your company have an adequate line of credit? No, we are working with our banks to increase our limit to $500,000.
Are you seeking additional credit sources? Yes, we are working with a leasing company.
Are you seeking a private placement? No
Are you planning to sell stocks or corporate bonds? No
Are you planning to do an IPO? Yes
Approximate date of announcement? June, 1997
What does your company plan to do with additional financing? We want to acquire a multimedia production company. We are also interested in acquiring a small book publisher in the business / financial / computer market.
Specify amount of financing. We want to issue 1 million shares of private stock at $15 per share.
Do you have a fallback plan if you do not receive funding, or if your funding is delayed? If we cannot complete an IPO we will continue to finance our growth from retained earnings.
Have you developed a Financing Plan? If so, attach a copy. No, we will be interviewing investment bankers in the near future.

continued . . .

Financial Information
Has your Financing / Business Plan been reviewed by an outside consultant or CPA to make sure that your assumptions are logical and consistent?
Our in-house counsel and controller have reviewed our business plan and agree that it is within our abilities.
Our plan has also been reviewed by our corporate bank's senior financing representative.

ATTITUDES, PRACTICES, AND PROCEDURES

Client-Centered™ Training may need to replace its current accounting system if it cannot support its international transactions.

Business Forecast Below (–) Equal (=) Above (+)	Next 6 Months	Next 24 Months	Next 36 Months
Sales	+	+	+
Profits	+	+	+
Margins	=	+	-
Overhead	+	+	+
Marketing Expenses	+	+	+
Cash Flow	-	=	=
Working Capital	=	-	+
Production Costs	=	-	-
Inventory Level	=	+	+
A/R Collections	-	=	=

continued . . .

Business Forecast Below (−) Equal (=) Above (+)	Next 6 Months	Next 24 Months	Next 36 Months
Pricing	=	-	-
Customer Support	-	=	+
Image / Quality	=	+	+
Staff Satisfaction	=	=	=
Customer Satisfaction	=	=	=

Financial Condition Next 6 Months	Less (%)	The Same	Greater (%)
Sales			12%
Net Income			6%
Production Costs			3%
Margins			7%
Overhead		No Change	
Cash	65,000.		
Collections			85,000.
Working Capital		No Change	
Investment in Inventory			75,000.

Note: You can use this report to help you manage your operations on an ongoing basis. For example, you might complete one worksheet to help forecast performance over the next six months, and additional worksheets to look out 9,12 and 18 months.

ATTITUDES, PRACTICES, AND PROCEDURES

Client-Centered™ Training's practice of financing growth from retained earnings may be impractical at this point because of its plan to open new markets and acquire multimedia businesses. Leasing may be an option to help C-CT finance IT purchases.

MARKET FACTORS

Every business is controlled by market factors that impact customers' buying decisions. These worksheets help you to identify these factors and see how they affect the business.

Market Factors	Key Factors
Industry	Professional education and business consulting
Type of Business	Training, Publishing
Geography	North America - expanding into Europe, Asia and South America
What is the history of your market?	Established in virtually all business markets. Growing at about 18% per year for the last ten years.
Why and how has it grown?	As the cost of doing business increases, it becomes more cost effective for our customers to leverage their personnel's capabilities with training seminars and workshops.
How stable is your market?	General economic factors may impact our sales; however, over a 12 month period our market is surprisingly stable.

continued . . .

Market Factors	Key Factors
What is the total size of your market?	Virtually every business with sales over $10 million is a prospect for our training services. Businesses with sales of over $2 million are prospects for our consulting services.
Number of units per year?	N/A
Revenue per year?	We estimate our market size to be about $350 million.
What percent (share) of your market do you control?	Less than 2%
Have any of your competitors been forced out of business recently? If so, why?	Yes, the Brain Trust went Chapter 11 last month. We believe it was because they were not able to develop new products fast enough.
Are there any major obstacles that may prevent you from realizing your market objectives?	We need to find employees who are professional, entrepreneurial, and self-motivated. We have had difficulty finding people with previous experience in our business.
How and when do you expect technological innovation to de-stabilize your market?	The Internet will enable companies to publish multimedia training courseware as soon as faster links - to stream video - are available. ISDN can provide this capability, but most of our clients are waiting for their phone companies to provide higher bandwidth DSL lines. We believe companies that are not publishing courseware on the Internet will be relegated to niche markets within five years.

continued . . .

Market Factors	Key Factors
What is the time-frame for your next technological "window of opportunity"?	We believe that we can offer our current products—repackaged on CD-ROMs—next year. This should give us a short window of opportunity (two year product cycle) to recoup our investment in multimedia, before we prepare our programs for the Internet.
Other	

ATTITUDES, PRACTICES, AND PROCEDURES

Client-Centered™ Training is aware of the impact that emerging multimedia and Internet technologies will have on its fundamental business model.

However, even though C-CT is anticipating these changes, it is concerned that its window of opportunity to take advantage of these opportunities is very narrow. If C-CT cannot recoup investment in multimedia training, it may not be able to fund the work it needs to do to prepare its training programs to take advantage of high-bandwidth Internet access in the future.

Emerging Market Factors That May Impact Your Business	What Are You Doing to Capitalize on These Factors?
Private and Public Educational Institutions	As colleges and universities begin to compete more aggressively for students, they are beginning to target professional education. At this point, we are not too concerned about this trend. However, as these institutions begin working with more business professionals, they will be able to provide a compelling alternative to our Executive Training Seminars.

continued . . .

Emerging Market Factors That May Impact Your Business	What Are You Doing to Capitalize on These Factors?
The Internet	We are planning to use our Web server to publish our courseware. We want to have this operational by next year. We are looking for a qualified Web master to help us manage this process.
Multimedia / CD-ROM Training	We are planning to acquire a multimedia company that has had experience working with companies in our business. We want to make all of our written materials available on CD-ROM by the middle of next year.
Satellite Broadcast Training	We are evaluating development of an infomercial to help us market our general business courseware. We need to learn more about this technology.
Growing awareness of Total Quality Management and ISO 9000 certification.	We will be evaluating the benefits of having our documentation group ISO 9000 certified next year. We have begun searching for the right TQM consultant to help us, if we decide to become certified.

Emerging market factors, such as consolidation of suppliers and emerging technologies, can dramatically impact your business. The time you invest anticipating these can help ensure the continued viability of your business.

ATTITUDES, PRACTICES, AND PROCEDURES

Managing the production of complex documents in a workgroup is very difficult to do with standard word processing applications.

Client-Centered™ Training should consider implementing a Document Management System to help manage production of its training materials.

PRODUCTS AND SERVICES

Every product that you develop and bring to market must be targeted to your customers' needs. Defining the strengths and weaknesses of your products will help you create an action plan for improving your competitive position in your market.

Product	Features	Benefits	Disadvantages
Training Seminars	Customized Modular	Meet specific client's needs	Time and money to develop custom programs
Consulting Services	Depth of Industry Experience Audit Program	Predictable outcome Can be done in phases	More expensive than doing training or audit with in-house personnel
Books and Training Guides	Concise, up-to-date Attractive format Inexpensive	Compelling to read Easy to understand Useful information	Not as effective as multimedia or live presentation

MARKET ANALYSIS

The market analysis worksheets spell out the number of units of a specific product that were produced over the past five years, how much revenue each specific product earned, and the percentage of the total market represented by the company's products.

Total Market (Product or Service)	Number of Units (Emerging Technology Training Programs)	Revenues
Last year	800	$8 million
This year	1400	$14 million
One year	2400	$24 million
Two years	3200	$32 million
Three years	4000	$40 million
Four years	5000	$50 million
Five years	6200	$62 million

Note: Use one table for each product or service.

- Where do these market estimates come from? For example, industry reports, internal analysis, etc.?

  Our forecast is based on user surveys and market estimates provided by the Big City Research Company. Our internal market data confirm these estimates.

- Are you confident that the information you have about your market is accurate and up-to-date?

  We are continually monitoring trends in our market, and are trying to stay abreast of new technology developments which may change our customers' expectations for our products and services.

Total Market Controlled	Total Number of Units	Units We Delivered	Percentage of Market
Last year	800	12	1.5%
This year	1400	28	2%
One year	2400	72	3%
Two years	3200	128	4%
Three years	4000	240	6%
Four years	5000	400	8%
Five years	6200	620	10%

- What do you base your future sales estimates on?

This forecast is based on our ability to do an IPO in two years to generate the capital we need to increase our brand awareness and attract new customers.

This forecast also assumes that we will be able to adopt emerging Internet technologies to provide products which are competitive with lower cost courseware provided by public and private educational institutions.

ATTITUDES, PRACTICES, AND PROCEDURES

Client-Centered™ Training is concerned that the Internet will obviate its yet-to-be launched multimedia business within 24 months. By anticipating the impact that the Internet will have on its fundamental business model, C-CT may be able to reposition its products quickly enough to gain a competitive advantage over those training companies and educational institutions that are reluctant to adopt Internet technology.

MARKET DIFFERENTIATION FACTORS

Businesses can differentiate themselves by many factors, including their products, their service level and the "value" they provide to their customers.

You can use the Market Differentiation Factors worksheet to help you analyze the value that your organization delivers to your customers.

Market Differentiation Factors
Marketing
We are using the Internet to help us attract and communicate with potential clients.
Sales / Distribution Channels
We target Fortune 5000 companies.
Product Line
We provide leading-edge training opportunities, courseware and books for successful professionals. We also provide strategic marketing consulting services.
Manufacturing
We currently outsource almost all manufacturing.
We outsource all color print services.
We can manufacture new training guides in eight to ten working days

continued . . .

Market Differentiation Factors
Service / Support
We provide custom training programs that are designed to meet our clients' specific needs and concerns.
We provide an unconditional guarantee that our training experience will match or exceed our program description as described in our marketing brochure and sales presentations.
Purchasing
We have relationships with several low-cost international suppliers.
We plan to reduce our dependence on outside printing services.
Research and Development
We work with outside subcontractors, which enables us to reduce our overhead, and to be responsive to customers who have larger projects than our in-house staff can manage.
Other

BUSINESS CYCLES

Markets evolve over time. How do you perceive your market, your company, your products and your competition, in terms of their "life cycle"?

Business Life Cycles	Startup	Growth	Mature	Decline
YOUR INDUSTRY OR MARKET		X		
YOUR COMPANY		X		

Product Life Cycles	Startup	Growth	Mature	Decline
Consulting Services		X		
Emerging Technology Seminars		X		
Business Development Seminars	X			
Books			X	
Training Guides		X	X	
Multimedia Materials		X		
Internet Publication	X			
Emerging Technology Newsletter	X			

Market Life Cycles	Startup	Growth	Mature	Decline
Fortune 5000 companies in the U.S.			X	
Mid-sized companies that need help with strategic planning		X		
Europe	X			
Asia	X			

Competitors' Life Cycles	Startup	Growth	Mature	Decline
Colleges			X	
Universities				X
Regional Training Firms		X		
Management Consulting Firms			X	

YOUR CUSTOMER

As markets become more global, it is essential to understand as much as possible about your customers' needs and expectations, and about their buying process.

Describe Your Customer
Describe your typical customer:
• Our typical training client is a division or business unit of a Fortune 5000 "technology-driven" company.
• Our principal contact is usually a VP/Director of Sales
• Our typical consulting client is a mid-size company with $5-500 million in revenues.
• Over 80% of our clients are in the computer industry.
• Our principal consulting contact is the President/CEO, or VP of Marketing/Business Development.
Who in your target customer's company makes the buying decision?
• Training Programs - VP of Sales and Marketing, Sales Manager, Marketing Manager
• Consulting Services - Company's Board, CEO, President, COO, VP Sales and Marketing, VP of Information Technology

continued . . .

Describe Your Customer

Describe a typical sales cycle for your products:

About 85% of our business is repeat business, or is new business that is generated by referrals.

We assign account managers to major accounts to prospect for new business opportunities.

We also advertise, use direct mail and very selective telemarketing to invite prospective customers to free seminars. We make sure that our marketing seminars provide as much value as possible to invited attendees.

We ask all contacts to describe their training requirements.

In most cases we generate a proposal and make a sales presentation to address our prospect's concerns.

Initial contact:

We are frequently contacted by former clients who refer us to their business associates.

Sales Process:

If our prospect is interested in scheduling a program, we have a preliminary meeting where we discuss their objectives and requirements. Then, we have a second meeting where we review our proposed agenda.

Request for Information:

If a prospect asks for information about our services, we send out a marketing packet and follow up with a telephone call within five working days to be sure that the prospect has all of the information needed. If the prospect is qualified, we schedule an initial meeting to discuss training requirements.

Request for Proposal or Quotation:

We usually do not respond to unsolicited Requests For Proposal. We specialize in custom program development, so we are not competitive with training companies that offer "pre-packaged" seminars.

Problem Analysis:

At our initial meeting we discuss our prospective customer's needs and provide samples of training materials.

We also provide references if appropriate.

continued . . .

Describe Your Customer

Who is involved in the selling process from your company?

The account manager is the "quarterback" for our team. Depending on the situation, we may have a senior manager support the sales process.

If a great deal of support materials will be developed we bring in one of our documentation specialists to review our client's requirements.

We do not bring any of our subcontractors into our accounts.

Average time frame for each step of your selling cycle:

Request for information to initial sales meeting: 1 to 3 weeks, depending on client's schedule.

Initial meeting to contract: 2 to 6 weeks depending on our client's concerns, and on the time needed to develop a proposal.

Contract to delivery: 6 to 12 weeks depending on client's needs.

Typical objections and concerns:

- Price - can't afford custom program development
- Time frame for delivery
- Want application-specific training
- Want to interview our presenter
- Concerned materials will be too advanced
- Client doesn't have time to "manage" outside consultants

Describe your sales tracking process (paper flow) in your organization:

1. Account manager forecasts top 10 prospects.
2. Account manager receives client's order for services.
3. Order is sent to sales manager.
4. Sales manager sends copies of order to: Production Manager, Training Scheduling Coordinator and Billing Department

continued . . .

Describe Your Customer
When was the last time your company sent out a customer satisfaction survey? July, 1996
Number of customers surveyed? 46
Number of responses? 43
Positive Response: Happy with deliverables
Negative Response: Want faster delivery - need programs scheduled with less than six weeks notice.
How could you shorten your organization's sales cycle: We need to schedule periodic meetings with our major accounts to help us learn about their training requirements, and to help us initiate new training opportunities. We are piloting a "training outsource" concept which will enable us to team an account manager and a training coordinator with our major clients to provide specialized services and to increase our knowledge of our client's business.

PURCHASE FACTORS

Customers base their buying decisions on various purchase factors. One customer, for example, might purchase computers because of their confidence in a trusted reseller, while another company might choose computers because of their compatibility with its existing computer equipment or because of the availability of specific features.

There is no "perfect" product for every customer's needs. In most cases, customers must trade off some level of performance or quality against their desire to solve their problem as inexpensively as possible.

Taking the time to understand which purchase factors your customers feel are most important will enable you to focus your product development and marketing efforts to anticipate and address their most important concerns.

Customer Purchase Factors	1 (not very important) to 5 (very important)
Reputation of Supplier	3
Personal References	4
Past Experience With Supplier	5
Size and Viability of Supplier	3
Range of Products from Supplier	2
Specific Capabilities or Functionality	4
Quality of Products	5
Perceived Value	5
Utility of Products	4
Style of Products	3
Availability - Delivery Time	3
Quality of Sales Personnel - Personal Rapport	2
Sales Presentations and Demonstrations	3
Marketing Message - Advertising	2
Quality of Support, Training, and Service	5
Third-Party Support	3
Proximity to Supplier and Support	4
Warranty	3
Price of Products - Financing Terms	3
Other	--
Other	--

CUSTOMER SATISFACTION

A recent study done for a division of American Airlines' parent company AMR, quantified the cost of poor customer service. The survey found that "One unhappy passenger tells nine to thirteen people about his or her bad experience. One happy flier tells just five people. Just 4% of unhappy customers complain. But for every person who complains, there are 24 unhappy customers who don't say anything. Of those who complain, 82% to 95% will do business with the company again if their problem gets solved quickly. But 75% to 90% of those 24 unhappy and uncomplaining customers will never do business with the company again."[5]

- When was the last time your company did a user satisfaction survey?

  Last August.

- What were the results of your user satisfaction survey?

  Generally very positive. See Average Ratings on Customer Satisfaction Form. (All of our major accounts responded. The survey was done by an outside research firm.)

Customer Satisfaction Survey Form	Rate 1 (not satisfied) to 5 (very satisfied)
Are you satisfied with our companies' products?	4
Are you satisfied with our companies' service?	5
Are you satisfied with our companies' sales representatives?	4
Are you satisfied with our companies' policies?	5
How do we compare to your company's other suppliers?	4

[5]Source: *USA Today*, May 21, 1996, page 10B

ATTITUDES, PRACTICES, AND PROCEDURES

Client-Centered™ Training provides a high level of customer service. Any technology, such as Internet e-mail, fax-on-demand or videoconferencing, which can help it communicate more easily with its clients will help it maintain this advantage.

COMPETITION

Virtually every business today faces competition for its customer's business. Your company's success will be primarily determined by your ability to respond to your customer's needs with a compelling sales message. Depending on your own market situation, your company may choose to differentiate itself from your competitors by focusing on price, service, style or any of the other factors listed in the Customer Purchase Factor worksheet.

For example, your company may employ a high price—high-service strategy against a discounter that is using a low price—low-service strategy. Smaller companies can often win market share against more established, better capitalized competitors by identifying and addressing their customer's major concerns, and by focusing their marketing efforts on a particular buying group, product segment, or geographic market region. IT systems can help companies provide this focus.

Competitive Forces
What markets have you targeted for future marketing efforts?
Europe and Asia
(Type of user, SIC Code, New Application, etc.)
We would like to focus our telemarketing on companies that have a (regional/territories) direct sales force.
We will be launching multimedia Training titles next February.
Why did you target these markets?
Europe and Asia are just beginning to appreciate the need for post-academic professional education.
We believe we can position our company as the leading (international) management training organization by being an early market participant.
We feel multimedia titles will enable us to take advantage of the Internet.

continued . . .

Competitive Forces

Entry Factors (for example, undercut market price to build market share.)

We want to maintain our "total quality" image. We plan to price our products accordingly in all new markets.

If our client is not willing to pay a premium for our service, we pass on its business.

Threat of substitution (for example, a CPA firm may offer computer services.)

We are concerned that public and private colleges and universities may become more aggressive in pursuing professional training opportunities.

We do not believe that this will pose a serious competitive threat as long as they continue to rely on academic resources.

Bargaining power of buyers (for example, you can play competitors to "bid-down" prices.)

Our clients are usually much more concerned with the quality of our deliverables than our consulting fees.

Our primary competition is ongoing business activities which make it difficult to schedule training programs.

Bargaining power of suppliers (for example, you could raise prices to reduce industry profitability.)

Our suppliers are continually raising prices. However, at this time we do not anticipate that this will significantly impact our profitability.

Margins on our books and training guides may be impacted next year if the cost of paper continues to escalate.

Rivalry among current competitors (see Competitive Strategies)

We compete primarily with our client's internal training groups - however, in most cases, our programs are perceived as being complementary to internal training programs.

Academic institutions pretend we do not exist.

We do not think our market has a high enough profile to attract the interest of large companies in related industries that are looking for expansion opportunities. However, this situation may change if any of the leading regional training companies are acquired by large consulting companies.

Competitive Strategies
Cost Leadership
We do not attempt to compete on price.
Differentiation (design or brand image, technology, distribution, features, customer service)
We have secured a position in our market as a leading supplier of custom training programs.
Focus (on a particular buying group, product segment or geographic area)
We target Fortune 5000 customers.
Our clients demand the very best training experience available.
Generic (a.k.a. all things to all customers)
We do not have the resources to be "all things to all customers." So we don't try to be.

ATTITUDES, PRACTICES, AND PROCEDURES

Client-Centered™ Training does not attempt to compete on price; however, C-CT's profitability is directly related to product development expenses and its cost of sales. Emerging technologies, such as color laser printers, can help C-CT provide a high-quality business image, and can help it support its "best services available for any price" market position.

Main Competitors in Product/Service Market Segment
Product / Service: Marketing and Technical Communications Consulting
Accounting Companies' Management Consulting Groups
Independent Industry Related Consultants
Research Firms
Trade Press / Analysts / Gurus
Product / Service: Client-Centered™ Training Seminars
Academic Institutions
Regional Training Companies

continued . . .

Main Competitors in Product/Service Market Segment
Internet-based Training Companies Multimedia Training Companies
Product / Service: Training Books and Guides Part-time MBA Programs Video Seminars / Executive Briefings Other Business Publications Newsletters

Advantages of Doing Business with Your Company	Advantages of Doing Business with Your Competitors
Our seminars are custom tailored to our customer's requirements.	Less expensive "seminar in a box" programs.
Highest quality product available.	Standard products are available off the shelf.
Custom training materials are prepared.	Basic courseware is good.
Highest quality presenters.	More readily available presenters.
Will work with customer to tailor product.	Does not require management's attention.
Depth of industry insight.	May have access to better market research. Cover more areas - such as finance.
Provide coverage in U.S.	Provide global coverage.
Provide books to back up seminars.	Provide multimedia training materials.

Marketing Activities	Expense High, Moderate, Low	Impact 1 (least effective) 5 (most effective)
Telemarketing	Moderate	3
Direct Mail (In-house)	Low	1
Direct Mail Service	Low	2
Direct FAX	Very Low	2
Seminars	High	5
Referral Program	No Cost	4
Press Relations	Moderate	2
Joint Marketing Activities	Varies	--
Print Advertising	High	2
Radio Advertising	N/A	--
Television Advertising	N/A	--
Internet Advertising	Low	1
Trade Show	High	4
Other Promotions		

ATTITUDES, PRACTICES, AND PROCEDURES

Advertising on the Internet is becoming less expensive; however, it is unclear whether it is very effective. As better Internet search tools become available, it will become less important for Client-Centered™ Training to build links from other frequently accessed sites to its own Web site.

BUSINESS DEVELOPMENT

You will need to expand your organization's information systems infrastructure as you take on new business opportunities. The following worksheets deal with marketing plans, distribution, sales factors, competitors, promotion, and budgets.

Marketing Plans
What new products or services would you offer if you had the capital to finance new ventures? Multimedia Products Video Training Seminars Prepackaged Technology Audit Guides
What new projects do you have planned? Review and repackage Dayton Associates training materials Evaluate multimedia opportunities Develop an Internet banner advertisement
Do you plan to release any new products in the next five months? Book on "Client-Centered™ Selling" Book on "Trade Show Selling" Book on "Time Management"
Do you plan to release any new products in the next six to twelve months? CD-ROM based Training Materials Executive Technology Briefing on the Internet Executive Technology Briefing on Network Computing
Do you plan on starting up a new business? We plan to acquire a multimedia production company, and bring all print services in-house.
Do you plan on opening new markets? Europe Asia
What advertising or press related activities do you have planned for the next six months? Print advertising in industry periodicals. Press tour to promote Technology Audit Workbook program.

continued . . .

Marketing Plans

What marketing materials, such as product brochures and white papers, do you plan to create over the next six months?

Client-Centered™ Training Programs Brochure

Client-Centered™ Selling Workshop Guide

Client-Centered™ Trade Show Selling Guide

White Paper on the Technology Audit Process

Executive Technology Briefing Brochure

What seminars, trade shows or other promotional activities do you plan to attend or sponsor over the next six months?

National Business Conference

Internet Conference

Big Computer Show

Manufacturer's Trade Symposium

National Training Association Conference

Do you have licenses or agreements in place to manufacture, distribute, market or resell any other company's products or services? Yes

Describe these agreements.

We have entered an agreement to publish and distribute Dayton Associates' training materials.

Are you involved in any joint ventures? Yes

Describe these joint ventures:

We plan to enter into a joint venture with our European distributor. It will localize and resell our products.

Are you working with any outside product developers or testers?

Yes, we use subcontractors to help develop custom materials.

Do you work with any outside training organizations? No

ATTITUDES, PRACTICES, AND PROCEDURES

Client-Centered™ Training can use remote access software and dial-in connections to provide its subcontractors with controlled access to its local area network.

Sales Factors	Sales Model
How many prospects do you have for your products and/or services?	We estimate about 15,000 for our training services. Our consulting prospect base is over 350,000 companies.
What is your cost per lead?	We do not really know. We think it is about $350.
What is your conversion rate from leads to sales?	We work with about 50 active and 350 inactive prospects. About 80% of active prospects become clients.
What percentage of your business comes from existing customers?	About 60%
How price sensitive are your established customers?	Our customers are not very price sensitive. Our competitor's customers are obviously more price sensitive!
Do you offer special financing terms?	Yes - we offer 30-90 days to customers in good standing
Would it be beneficial to partner with a financial institution, lease partner or other financial services provider?	We partner with a financial services company to help us finance large projects.

Distribution Model

Do you use the same distribution channels as your competitors?

Basically yes. We sell training services directly to major corporations through our East and West coast sales offices.

We do not understand distribution channels in Europe and Asia so we will be working with our marketing partners.

If not, why have you chosen the distribution channels you are currently using?

Advantages

Disadvantages

If so, have you considered using alternative distribution channels to increase sales of your products?

Yes, we are considering working with regional CPA firms that can introduce us to technology-driven clients.

We are also considering partnering with industry-specific consulting firms in areas where we do not have direct sales representatives.

Channel Matrix	% of Seminar Sales for Industry	% of C-CT Seminar Sales	% of Consulting Sales for Industry	% of C-Ct Consulting Sales
Direct Mail	60	22	15	12
Telemarketing	6	3	2	3
Outside Sales	30	75	80	85
Retail	2	--	--	--
Distributor	--	--	--	--

continued . . .

Channel Matrix	% of Seminar Sales for Industry	% of C-CT Seminar Sales	% of Consulting Sales for Industry	% of C-Ct Consulting Sales
OEM	--	--	--	--
Infomercial	1	--	--	--
Internet	1	--	--	--
Other	--	--	--	--
Other	--	--	--	--

Channel Margins	Percentage Gross Margin	Percentage of Sales	Total Revenue
Direct Mail	50	12	170,000
Telemarketing	60	3	30,000
Outside Sales	80	85	1,800,000
Retail	60	--	--
Distributor	N/A	--	--
OEM	N/A	--	--
Infomercial	55	--	0
Internet	85	--	0
Other	--	--	--

Reseller Analysis	% of Reseller Leads	% of Company Leads
Sales Representative	N/A	100
Reseller	N/A	N/A
Distributor (Books)	90	10
Other: Consultants	N/A	100

Competitive Channel Matrix % of Sales	State College	Regional Training Firm	Independent Consultant	Client-Centered Training
Direct Mail	80	60	25	12
Telemarketing	5	15	40	3
Outside Sales	--	20	15	85
Retail	--	--	--	--
Distributor	--	--	--	--
OEM	--	--	--	--
Infomercial	--	--	--	--
Internet	10	5	20	--
Other	5	--	--	--
Other	--	--	--	--

Distribution
Describe the geographic region(s) including countries, states, regions or cities where your products are sold: *We are marketing our products throughout North America.*
Do you plan to expand distribution of your products? *We are planning to expand into Europe and Asia next year. We are also partnering with a company in South America.*
Are your sales seasonal, or tied to any other external factors? *Our executive technology briefings are tied to interest in emerging technologies. Our typical "window of opportunity" is about 9 months.* Do you control pricing to your customers? *Yes. We are in a specialized market - custom program development, and work with clients who are motivated to develop the highest quality programs.*
Are you actively engaged in developing new markets for your products and services? *Yes, we are developing a new training program every two to three months.*
If you are developing new products, have you identified any customers, resellers and/or other developers that would be willing to partner with you to specify needs, develop prototypes, or provide product testing or pre-release marketing services? *Yes. We want to partner with or acquire a media company as soon as possible. We are also interested in partnering with a video production company.*

PROMOTION

The promotional model details the specific ways in which a company advertises its products and services.

Promotional Model
Do you have brochures which describe your organization's mission statement and strategic objectives?
No. But we are planning to create a white paper on our corporate objectives.
Do you have brochures which describe your organization's products and services?
Yes. We have brochures on our training programs and on our consulting services.
Do you have brochures which describe your sales program?
Not specifically. Our sales representatives receive monthly bulletins which cover sales policies, upcoming events and other sales information.
Do you have a Reseller Kit which includes all of the information that your sales representatives and/or resellers need to promote and sell your products?
No, but we plan to create one for our European distributor.
Do you have a Service Kit which includes all of the information that third-party service organizations need to service and support your products?
N/A
Do you provide marketing aids, such as portable trade show booths, sales presentations and promotional videos to your resellers?
Yes. We have a brief video presentation which includes commendations from major customers and a brief explanation of how we develop custom training programs. We also have a portable 10'X10' trade show booth which we loan out to our joint marketing partners.
Do you have an Advertising Plan?
No. We periodically place space advertisements in industry trade publications. Our PR agency will be proposing a plan to us next month.
Are Corporate Communications handled by an outside agency?
We work with the Seattle Press Relations and Corporate Communications Company.
Do you have regular meetings with outside service organizations which support your:

continued . . .

Promotional Model
• Marketing: No • Advertising: Yes • Press Relations: Yes • Corporate Communications: Yes • Stockholder Relations: N/A • Other:
Who is responsible for your company's product packaging? *Vice President of Sales and Marketing and Director of Marketing*
Who is responsible for maintaining your corporate identity? *Our Director of Marketing*
What components, such as your company's logo, do you consider to be important to maintaining your corporate identity? *Client-Centered™ Training, Client-Centered™ Selling, corporate logo, tag-line: "Today's Marketing Technology", and style guide for all training materials.*
Do you believe that your corporate identity and the image it presents to your market are consistent with your company's business objectives? *Yes* Who is responsible for managing your identity? *Vice President of Sales and Marketing*
Do you have a formal licensing program to support and maintain your corporate identity? *Not yet. We may offer some type of training franchise in the future for resellers interested in presenting our "packaged" seminars.*

ATTITUDES, PRACTICES, AND PROCEDURES

Client-Centered™ Training has not specified how it will budget IT resources to support its new projects. It is very unlikely that C-CT's IT department will be able to support these new projects with its current IT budget.

Promotion	Effectiveness (Number of Leads Generated)	Expense (Cost per Lead)
Brochures / Handbills	5	$3,000.
Print Advertising	75	$25,000.
Radio Advertising	--	--
Television Advertising	--	--
Internet Advertising	--	--
Seminar Programs	210	$12,000.
Direct Mail	1200	$20,000.
Telemarketing	420	$15,000.
Trade Shows	258	$25,000.
Press Releases	--	--
Press Conferences	--	--
Press Tours	--	--
Other	--	--

ATTITUDES, PRACTICES, AND PROCEDURES

Client-Centered™ Training may be able to reduce its sales expenses by automating sales lead follow-up.

Promotion Budgets	Percentage of Competitors' Budgets	Percentage of Your Company's Budget
Brochures / Handbills	5	3
Print Advertising	5	25
Radio Advertising	--	--
Television Advertising	--	--
Internet Advertising	5	--

continued . . .

Promotion Budgets	Percentage of Competitors' Budgets	Percentage of Your Company's Budget
Seminar Programs	10	12
Direct Mail	60	20
Telemarketing	5	15
Trade Shows	10	25
Press Releases	--	--
Press Conferences	--	--
Press Tours	--	--
Other	--	--
Other	--	--
Other	--	--

BUSINESS TERMS

The business terms worksheet ranks each purchase conern according to its importance to the customer on a scale of 1 (not important) to 5 (very important).

Business Terms	Importance to Customers 1 (not important) to 5 (very important)
Credit Terms	2
Credit Cards	1
Returns	3
Refunds	3
Pick-up and Delivery	4
Expedited Shipping	5
Quantity Discounts	5

continued . . .

Business Terms	Importance to Customers 1 (not important) to 5 (very important)
Bundled (Packaged) Pricing	5
Warranty	3
Select Principal Contact	4
Select Trainer	4
Other	--

Note: use one form for each product, territory, major account.

SERVICE AND SUPPORT

The service and support worksheets describe both internal and external resources.

Service/Support/Consulting Model
Do you maintain a support organization? Yes
Do you work with any third-party support organizations? Yes, we partner with regional consulting firms.
Who does your Support Manager report to? Vice President of Sales and Marketing
Is support a profit center for your business? Yes
How much revenue was generated by your support activities? $811,000.
How much cost was allocated to your support activities? $453,000.
What profit or (loss) did you incur in the last six months? $138,000.
What profit or (loss) do you forecast for the next twelve months? $262,000.
Are support tasks scheduled and tracked using an automated project tracking and management system? We use Microsoft Project and Microsoft Schedule+ to help us manage our accounts.

continued . . .

Service/Support/Consulting Model
Have you audited your Support Department in the last 12 months? No
Do you send out customer surveys to evaluate your customers' satisfaction with your support services? Yes
Date of survey: February, 1997
Comments: Our clients are satisfied with our services - but they would like us to provide better payment terms.

Service Issues	Issue
How many employees provide customer service / support?	10
How do you bill their time / work?	Hourly or on support contracts
What percent of customer support time is billable?	About 40%
What is your billing rate for service? Is this rate low, average or high for your industry?	$85.00 - $125.00 / hour Average for industry
Who determines billable hours?	Vice President of Sales
Are support services automated?	Yes, all support personnel are on a network
Are support requirements cyclical?	No
Is the service organization a profit center?	Yes - but marginally
When was the last time you evaluated the cost of providing customer service?	Last year
Who is your service / support manager?	Production Manager

continued . . .

Service Issues	Issue
Who does the service / support manager report to?	Vice President of Operations
Do you have outstanding service contracts with third-party service organizations?	No

DISTRIBUTION

The manner in which a company distributes its products or services, once they are available, is critical to its success. This worksheet details the important aspects of distribution.

Reseller Model
How do you select sales representatives?
Personal qualities, previous experience in industry, Internet-hosted testing service qualification.
How do you select resellers?
Previous experience in industry, reputation, previous level of success, geographical territory, referrals, level of commitment.
How do you select distributors?
Geographical territory, previous experience in industry, reputation, previous level of success, referrals, level of commitment.
How do you select third-party service (consultants) representatives?
Personal qualities, previous experience in industry, Internet-hosted testing service qualification.
Do you have a sales and service training program in place?
No. We may offer one in the future.

PRODUCTION ISSUES

Production issues include all of the components of the workflow process.

Production Issues
Do you have adequate production resources?   *We want to bring most of our printing in-house over the next two years.*
Personnel   Specify areas which are understaffed.   *Our Training Guide production group is understaffed.*
Equipment   Describe production load limitations.   *We can only seat 20 people in our main training room.*   Describe any capital (mission-critical) equipment nearing the end of its useful life.   *Our network laser printers need to be replaced within six months.*   Do you have a back-up plan for equipment failure?   *We need additional portable computers and computer presentation equipment. We do not have an adequate disaster recovery program if our main file server crashes.*
Inventory Control (Describe your inventory control system.)   *We are running Inventory Management software on a Windows/NT server which is connected to our LAN.*   *All of our training materials are warehoused at our East coast and West coast sales offices.*
Do you have a backup plan to obtain products or supplies which are difficult to obtain, on allocation, or provided by a sole supplier?   *Our Production Manager is working on a formal purchasing plan.*
Do you have any plans to improve your inventory control system?   *We plan to begin bar coding all of our training materials next quarter.*

continued . . .

Production Issues
Shipping / Warehousing (Describe your shipping procedures.)
All materials are shipped from our sales offices directly to our customers.
We use Air Express for all expedited orders.
Do you experience difficulty shipping product during peak periods?
No
Do you have any plan to improve your shipping procedures?
Yes. Bar coding our inventory will help us improve turnaround time in our warehouse.

ATTITUDES, PRACTICES, AND PROCEDURES

Client-Centered™ Training could implement notebook computers with docking stations to help it improve the productivity of employees who spend time away from their desks, or who occasionally work at home.

The price of notebook computers has declined significantly over the last eighteen months, and current models provide adequate processor speeds, short and long-term memory storage and ergonomics. They account for over 25% of new PC sales.

Quality Control
How does your quality control compare to your competitors?
We target our programs at the high end of the market. We believe that they are the best available.
We certify all of our trainers and program support specialists.
Are you ISO 9000 certified?
No.
Would ISO 9000 certification help you market your products?
We believe it would, but we have not researched this yet. The European distributors we have talked with have asked us about our plans.
Do you have a plan in place to become ISO 9000 certified?
We are considering getting certification for our documentation group next year.
If we decide to work towards ISO certification, we will hire an outside consultant to help us through the process.

PURCHASING ISSUES

Purchasing issues include how and where to buy raw materials, who to use as suppliers and how to obtain adequate order fulfillment.

Purchasing Issues
Describe your purchase process.
We write up an RFP and submit it to at least three established suppliers.
The suppliers' bids are compared and a recommendation is submitted to our controller with the department manager's recommendations or concerns.
A letter notifying the chosen supplier is drafted and a budget is established.
Purchases are made with company Purchase Orders.
Department managers may sign POs up to $5,000. POs over $5,000 must be approved by our Controller, VP Operations or President.
Do you have any sole source suppliers?
Yes. We are concerned about our network consultants - Connect It. They do not have much experience with Wide Area Networks.
We are in the process of sending out an RFP for our network enhancements. We plan to use another supplier for this work.
Do you have a contingency plan in place if your supply for critical products is interrupted temporarily?
Our contingency plan for backup computer and network services is currently the Yellow Pages. We are trying to find backup and disaster service providers.
Also, our binder supplier Quick Save is the only local supplier for the type of binders we use for our seminars. We are trying to locate another supplier out of state.
Are you vulnerable / at risk because of unfavorable business relations with any of your sole source suppliers?
No - there are no competitive issues.

continued . . .

Purchasing Issues
Are your purchasing systems automated?
We track our POs with our Accounting System.
In the future we would like to move our purchasing system to our Intranet server and implement an electronic forms-based purchase requisition application.
Have you implemented EDI to support any of your customer's or supplier's order entry requirements?
We would like to implement an EDI system once we have our European and Asian distributors in place. However, this is not a high priority for us at this point.

ATTITUDES, PRACTICES, AND PROCEDURES

Client-Centered™ Training should consider automating its Purchase Order system as an Intranet application. Rapid Application Development tools which support Internet protocols are available that can help C-CT support its workflow requirements.

Primary Suppliers	Products or Services	Is Supplier Your Sole Source?	Purchased Amount Year to Date
Alan Printing	Printing	No	$110,000
NW Printer	Printing	No	$71,000.
Big Printer	Bindery	No	$65,000.
Copy Place	Copy Service	No	$32,000.
Computer All	Computers	No	$41,000.
Fast Connect	Network	Yes	$28,000.
Media Place	Media	Yes	$23,000.
Quick Save	Binders	Yes	$17,000.
Travel Now	Travel	No	$213,000.

continued . . .

Primary Suppliers	Products or Services	Is Supplier Your Sole Source?	Purchased Amount Year to Date
Office Repair	Fix Machines	Yes	$7,000.
Telephone Co.	Phone Service	Yes	$41,000.
Document It	Subcontractor	No	$114,000.
Write Now	Subcontractor	No	$21,000.

Outside Contractors
Administration Tasks
We do not use outside contractors in this area.
Production Tasks
We subcontract production work to our printer, copy center, and media supplier. We also work with subcontractors on custom training programs.
Order Fulfillment
We contract with Air Express to handle all priority shipments. They work directly with our East and West coast sales offices.
Operations Tasks
We are using a direct mail company to help us launch our new seminar program.

ATTITUDES, PRACTICES, AND PROCEDURES

Client-Centered™ Training might be able to save money by contracting with Federal Express or another carrier which can provide on-line pickup scheduling and package tracking.

Order Fulfillment and Purchasing Tasks
What is your average time for order fulfillment? 11 days
Do you expedite rush or special orders? Yes
Do you use a private carrier to handle rush or expedited orders? Air Express
Do you ever need to postpone order fulfillment because of production backlogs, out-of-stock inventory items, lack of equipment capacity, or other issues? Yes, we are having problems scheduling print runs.
Do seasonal or peak loads cause bottlenecks? We have had problems in March--our busiest month.
Do you hire additional personnel to handle seasonal or peak loads? Yes, we rely on our subcontractors.
Do you outsource work (e.g. a fulfillment company) to help you handle peak loads? We use our direct mail service to help us fulfill requests for information. Orders are forwarded to our East and West coast sales offices.
Do you have a formal bidding process in place with your subcontractors? Yes, we send out an RFP for all major projects.

ATTITUDES, PRACTICES, AND PROCEDURES

Client-Centered™ Training's Order Entry system could be interfaced with Microsoft Office using Microsoft Visual Basic to enable C-CT to automatically generate faxes and electronic mail messages to report order status to customers.

SALES FORECASTS AND ANALYSIS

SALES FORECASTS

Accurate sales forecasts enable a business to allocate its resources efficiently. They are usually expressed in dollar volumes and number of units; they often include the names of specific accounts that are expected to close, and the degree of certainty the account manager has that their predictions will come to pass.

Sales forecasts are usually based on a combination of factors, including:

- Number of active prospects
- Outstanding sales proposals
- Anticipated reorders
- Historical sales data
- Previous account sales history

Sales Planning	Responsibility
Who is responsible for generating Sales Forecasts?	Bob Jones
Forecast Frequency	Monthly
Forecast Accuracy	Our forecasts are within 35% of actual sales. We need to forecast more conservatively.
Who is responsible for generating Budgets?	Nancy Dawson
Budget Frequency	Quarterly
Budget Accuracy	We usually stay within 6% of our budget. Marketing budgets are indexed to sales revenues.

Sales Forecast
(Business Unit / Sale Team / Other)

Salesperson: *Thomas Butler*
Territory: *Southeast*
Date: *June, 1997*

Top 10 Prospects		Revenue	Percent Confidence
1	ABC Co.	15,000.	99
2	Big Sky	20,000.	99
3	Lazy Day	18,000.	90
4	Pay Out	15,000.	90
5	So Long	16,000.	80
6	Pay Day	10,000.	80
7	Out A Here	24,000.	60
8	The Way	19,000.	55
9	Good Buy	11,000.	50
10	End Game	14,000.	40

Lower Priority Prospects:

Southeast Distributors	11,000.
Pick One Now	29,000.
Hard Sale	15,000.

Total Revenue Forecast for Period: $68,000.

Sales Forecast by Product by Period	1	2	3	4	5	6	7	8
Number of Units: Multimedia Programs	6	20	25	35	50	75	125	150
Revenue $1,000's	9	30	37.5	52.5	75	112.5	187.5	225
Profit $1,000's	0	0	0	0	0	40	80	150

SALES ANALYSIS

Overly conservative projections can lead to product shortages, if the production department reduces its output to match sales forecasts. And "blue sky" projections can lead to cash flow problems, if a company purchases additional raw materials, ramps production, or increases overhead to support an overstated demand for product.

Customer Sales Analysis by Period	1	2	3	4	5	6	7	8
Number of Units Purchased by ABC Distributing	800	850	200	700	1400	600	800	1100
Revenue Generated $1,000's	8	8.5	2	7	14	6	8	11
Profit Generated $1,000's	4	4.5	1	3.5	7	3	4	5.5

Sales Territory Analysis by Period	1	2	3	4	5	6	7	8
Training Seminars Sold in the Southeast	14	17	12	9	24	29	18	31
Revenue Generated $1,000's	140	170	120	90	240	290	180	310
% of Total Revenue	7	8.5	6	4.5	12	14.5	9	15.5
% Change Same Period Last Yr.	+38	+45	–8	+4	+82	+64	+45	+72
Profit Generated $1,000's	60	90	40	10	130	160	100	190
% of Total Profit	7	8.5	6	4.5	12	14.5	9	15.5
% Change from Last Period	+38	+45	–8	+4	+82	+64	+45	+72

ATTITUDES, PRACTICES, AND PROCEDURES

In the example, the percentages of total revenue and profit are equal, because Client-Centered™ Training does not allocate expenses between selling seminars and other activities, such as providing consulting services.

Product Sales Analysis by Period	1	2	3	4	5	6	7	8
Number of Books Sold	2900	3150	3300	2100	2400	3700	2900	2700
Revenue Generated $1,000's	29	31.5	33	21	24	37	29	27
% of Total Revenue	14.5	15.5	11.5	10.5	12	18.5	14.5	13.5
% Change from Last Period	+6	+11	+4	+23	+15	+19	+17	+16
Profit Generated $1,000's	17	21	22	11	13	23	21	18
% of Total Profit	14.5	15.5	11.5	10.5	12	18.5	14.5	13.5
% Change from Last Period	+6	+11	+4	+23	+15	+19	+17	+16

Business Risk Factors	1 (not prepared) to 5 (very prepared)
• Inability to raise funds to support business operations	4
• Lose credit line	3

continued . . .

Business Risk Factors	1 (not prepared) to 5 (very prepared)
• New hardware and systems software	3
• Enabling technologies such as electronic messaging and EDI	2
• New competitors	3
• Loss of key customers	2
• Price wars	4
• Decline in market demand	3
• Distribution channel conflicts	5
• Increased production costs	4
• Increased support costs	4
• Supplier delays	2
• Increase in cost of raw materials	3
• Loss of key suppliers	3
• New or stronger competitors	4
• Product delays	4
• Increase personnel costs	4
• Loss of key personnel	1
• Employee burnout	2
• Loss of key distributors or resellers	3
• Quality assurance problems	4
• Government regulations	4
• Corporate theft	1
• Fire, earthquake and other natural disaster	1
• Ineffective sales and marketing programs	3
• Product support problems (liability, etc.)	2

continued . . .

Business Risk Factors	1 (not prepared) to 5 (very prepared)
• Internal attack on information systems	1
• External attack on information systems	1
• Delayed or unsuccessful research and development	2
• Impact of emerging technology on business model	2

ATTITUDES, PRACTICES, AND PROCEDURES

Client-Centered™ Training has not identified the declining cost of delivering multimedia courseware as a potential risk factor. However, low cost CD-ROM authoring tools and Internet publishing may lower the cost of entry into some of C-CT's markets enough to encourage new training companies to publish their courseware in digital form.

Whether or not these competitive products are of the same quality as C-CT's products, C-CT will face increasing marketing costs if it wants to maintain its market position as the premium supplier of custom business training services.

AUDITOR'S RECOMMENDATIONS

This final worksheet provides an overview of the auditor's recommendtions after the completion of the business audit worksheets. It is typically a work-in-progress, and can be modified as new information becomes available.

Auditor's Recommendations
Note: This worksheet provides an executive level summary of the auditor's recommendations. It is not intended to replace the auditor's comprehensive IT Audit Report.

1. Client-Centered Training is planning to use the Internet to help it market its training products and consulting services.

    C-CT should consider implementing an Internet gateway on its LAN to support communications with its subcontractors, business partners and customers.

---

continued . . .

Auditor's Recommendations
Note: This worksheet provides an executive level summary of the auditor's recommendations. It is not intended to replace the auditor's comprehensive IT Audit Report.

C-CT should also consider migrating its existing network and workgroup applications to Internet protocols. This would enable it to leverage its multimedia production capabilities.

2. Billing and A/R costs are in line with industry expectations. There would be very little advantage in outsourcing these applications.

3. After C-CT has implemented its Intranet server, it should consider implementing a Purchase Order system which supports EDI. This application could support electronic forms for internal purchase requisitions and could be developed for an Intranet server.

4. C-CT's IT personnel's skills are in line with expectations. However, the organization needs to recruit technical personnel that have experience developing and maintaining Intranet applications and commercial Internet Web sites.

5. C-CT needs to develop IT budgets which reflect its planned expansion into Europe, Asia and South America, and its intent to use the Internet to develop an alternate sales and product support channel. We recommend a complete IT Budget review.

The IT Audit process is covered in Chapter 7.

INFORMATION SYSTEMS AUDIT WORKSHEETS

The term "information technology" is sometimes used interchangeably with information systems. But from our perspective, IT refers more broadly to the information systems, and all of the system's users inside and outside of the organization.

INFORMATION TECHNOLOGY SYSTEMS

The common element running through every aspect of IT analysis, implementation and management is support for the information needs of the system's users. Many business managers think of IT systems in terms of inputs, processes and outputs. But every aspect of IT systems is predicated on human interfaces.

INPUTS

- Business Problems
- Structured Information (Data)
- Unstructured Information (Documents, Images)
- Instructions
- System Users

PROCESSES

- Programs (Software Applications)
- Hardware
- Data Storage
- Data Communications

- Graphical User Interface
- System Users

OUTPUTS

- Reports
- Solutions
- Graphics
- Calculations
- Multimedia
- System Users

In addition to inputs, processes and outputs, IT systems must have a feedback or control component. This feedback drives the decision making process, and can directly impact business operations, productivity and profitability.

FEEDBACK—CONTROL

- Reports
- Business Managers (Decision Makers)

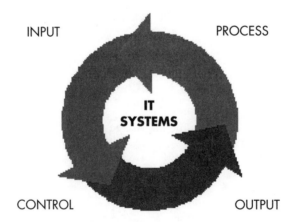

Taken together, these components enable IT Systems to support a constellation of critical response activities, such as: productivity, quality control, business strategy, managing the corporate culture, decision making, customer service, information access, business reengineering, developing new business opportunities and gaining competitive advantage.

ANALYZING IT SYSTEMS

There are many ways to characterize IT systems. The most common way is to describe them based on an organizational or functional "view," or on a "view" of operational support provided by the system.

ORGANIZATIONAL VIEW

- Enterprise level

- Business unit level

- Department level

- Workgroup level

It is critical that IT systems be designed to support user requirements at all levels of the organization. For example, enterprise level requirements for security and control must be enabled at the business unit, departmental and workgroup levels.

FUNCTIONAL AREA

- Finance

- Sales and marketing

- Research and development

- Manufacturing

- Production

- Distribution

- Human resources

- Facilities management

- Communications

- Other departments

IT systems must provide the specific functional requirements needed to improve productivity and lower operating costs in each area of the enterprise.

For example, systems used in research and development often have totally different requirements than those used in production. Nevertheless, the more interoperable these systems are, the easier it will be to manage system components and communications between these functional areas.

FUNCTIONAL SUPPORT (CAPABILITIES)

Many different types of specialized IT systems are interconnected to comprise an enterprise-wide IT infrastructure, which supports the requirements of all system users.

- Transaction processing system—TPS supports mission-critical business transaction processing.

- Management information system—MIS supports line of business managers.

- Office automation system—OAS supports office workers.

- Group support system—GSS supports people working in groups.

- Executive information system—EIS supports executive decision making.

- Decision support system—DSS supports managers and analysts.

- Intelligent support system—(Artificial Intelligence) ISS supports knowledge workers using expert systems and neural networks.

- Communications system—CS supports communication between all system users and system resources.

Type of System	People Supported
Strategic Systems [EIS/ESS]	Senior Managers
Staff Support [DSS]	Professional, Knowledge Workers
Managerial Systems [MIS]	Middle Managers
Operational Systems [TPS]	Line Managers, Operators
Office Automation Systems [OAS]	Clerical Staff
Communication Systems [CS]	System Users
Information Infrastructure [RDBMS]	Internal / External System Users

INFORMATION SYSTEMS ARCHITECTURE

An information systems architecture is also used to classify IT systems.

- *Mainframe*—Dominant IT architecture until late 1980's, characterized by a centralized data store and "dumb" terminals (user workstations); this architecture was extended to include intelligent PC workstations in the mid-1980s.

- *Minicomputer*—Scaled down mainframe computer architecture used to support small companies and departments of larger organizations; minicomputers are now being replaced by powerful PC servers.

- *Workstation*—Powerful microcomputer-based systems developed with proprietary hardware and software components, compete with high-end de facto standard Intel processor-based PC servers.

- *Personal Computer (PC)*—Dominant microcomputer-based platform; many organizations rely exclusively on PCs connected on networks to support their IT requirements.

- *Network Computer (NC)*—"Client" workstation that is specifically designed to run an Internet browser and component software downloaded from an Internet or Intranet server; NCs may be replaced by inexpensive PCs, or they may evolve into inexpensive, multipurpose "appliances" such as cellular telephones which have built-in displays and the ability to download Internet mail.

- *Distributed System*—A combination of different computer systems connected on a computer network.

IS architecture does not always map well to an organization's IT strategy, because IT technology is evolving so rapidly. For example, PCs employing SMP or clustering architecture have satisfied the need to install proprietary mini- and mainframe computer systems for many mission-critical department-level applications. And legacy mini- and mainframe computers are often used as application servers in distributed computing systems.

IT "VIEWS" ARE STRATEGIC TOOLS

Each "view" of your IT system is a tool that you can use to help you align your IT strategies with your business objectives. For example, if your organization's sales (Functional Area View) are distributed across different regional offices (Organizational View), your sales information will also be distributed between those regional offices. In this type of situation, it is usually cost effective to employ a distributed computing architecture, which enables the remote offices to access the information that they need to support their selling activities, and the centralized management and reporting functions that senior management needs to control its operations (Functional Support View).

ALIGNING IT SYSTEMS WITH BUSINESS NEEDS

As an auditor, you will need to determine whether the underlying information systems architecture is consistent with your client's business needs. The only way that you can do this is to first understand your client's business, and to then "visualize" the best way to support each class or type of system user.

For example, businesses often use relational database management systems (RDBMSs) to support high-volume online transaction processing (OLTP) requirements, and use an executive information system (EIS) to access, view and report business information that senior managers need to facilitate their strategic planning.

Executive information systems cannot work efficiently with huge database files. So an auditor might recommend that a client implement a data warehouse which contained a subset (summary information) of its OLTP database's files (detail information) to support its decision support requirements.

NORMALIZING AN IT INFRASTRUCTURE

"Normalizing" your client's IT Systems infrastructure requires eliminating unnecessary systems, reducing the number of disparate systems, and implementing de facto standard computer and communication APIs whenever possible. This is usually the most direct way to reengineer your client's IT systems to reduce costs, improve productivity and provide competitive advantage.

However, in some cases, such as the data warehouse example, it may be necessary to implement additional systems to support specific user requirements.

In another situation, office workers who have been teamed in workgroups to handle specific jobs may need data communication and information-sharing applications to support their work.

The less procedural and the more collaborative an application is, the more difficult it is to visualize whether or not it will be cost effective to automate, the harder it will be to install, implement and support, and the more difficult it will be for users to adapt to their own working style and expectations.

We never said it would be easy but you must understand your client's IT requirements, and have a thorough understanding of how IT systems can help your client address its needs before you can make any useful recommendations.

STRATEGIC IT PLANNING

STEP 1:

Define your client's IT requirements based on an organizational view, a functional area view, and a view of support provided by the system.

STEP 2:

Map your client's user requirements to its existing IT systems.

STEP 3:

"Normalize" your client's IT systems.

- Standardize hardware, software, and network systems whenever possible.
- Eliminate any unnecessary systems.
- Reduce the number of disparate systems.
- Implement de facto standard computer and communication APIs whenever possible.

STEP 4:

Validate your client's IT Strategy to achieve.

- *Pervasive Computing*—where every system user and every client processor can access every system resource at any time, from anywhere as required to support business objectives
- *Interoperability*—where every system object, including programs, services, and data can be shared by every system user and every system resource as required to support business objectives
- *Maximum Usefulness*—where every system provides maximum interoperability, scalability, modularity (component software), flexibility, data accessibility, portability, connectivity and maintainability as required to support evolving business requirements and objectives

STEP 5:

Propose an action plan.

- Evaluate emerging technologies

- Propose modifications and/or enhancements to existing IT systems

- Evaluate risk factors

- Deliver IT audit report to client

STEP 6:

Support implementation of recommendations.

VALIDATING YOUR IT STRATEGY

Most organizations' IT systems do not support pervasive computing, achieve inter-operability or provide maximum usefulness. Depending on the impact that emerging technologies have on your fundamental business model, you may need to replace or reengineer your IT infrastructure to align your IT strategies with your short- and long-term business objectives.

For example, in the financial services area, many firms are implementing Internet sites to handle commercial transactions. Companies that do not reengineer their IT systems to support network computing are in danger of losing customers as their market shifts from one-on-one personal selling to lower-cost direct (self-inflicted) electronic market transactions.

Network computing is an emerging technology, and is replete with problems, such as securing data transmission. Nonetheless, competitive pressures are driving financial services to begin adapting their legacy systems to operate with Internet-linked customers.

Fortunately, IT managers have a "once in an IT paradigm shift" opportunity to leverage senior managers' interest in the Internet to sell them the IT budgets they need to align their "next-generation" systems with their organizations' longer-term business objectives.

DEFINING CLIENT'S OBJECTIVES

It is important to define your objectives before beginning an information systems audit.

Key Objectives for Commissioning This Audit[6]
Objective 1
Evaluate current IT infrastructure to determine whether or not it is consistent with our business objectives.
Objective 2
Evaluate whether or not our current IT budget is in line with other businesses in our industry. Determine where we may achieve cost savings without reducing our current service level.
Objective 3
Evaluate whether or not it is advantageous to outsource our billing and receivables applications.
Objective 4
Evaluate our senior IT personnel's technical skills.
Objective 5
Evaluate the impact of the Internet on our business model.
Evaluate the feasibility of using an Intranet server to support workgroup computing applications.

SYSTEMS IMPLEMENTATION

Automated systems are generally installed and implemented by trained IT professionals in larger organizations, and by "PC power users" in departmental workgroups which do not have access to help desk personnel.

In smaller companies, systems are usually installed and implemented by outside consultants or system integrators, and maintained by a LAN administrator or PC

---

[6] A client's objectives for the business and information systems sections of an IT Audit may or may not be the same.

power user. Application data is usually maintained by primary application users. The example IS organization chart provides a top-down look at how many IS departments are structured.

Typical IS Organization Chart

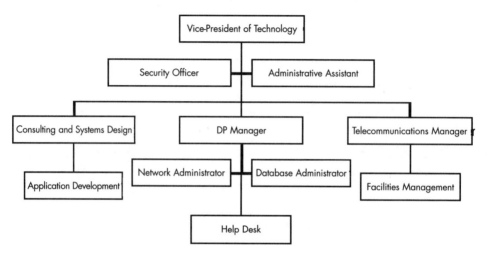

The information systems audit begins with basic facts about the IT department and the effectiveness of the systems currently in place.

Information Systems Personnel Issues
Attach a detailed organization chart of your client's IT department.
See IS Department organization chart above.
Are all IT positions currently filled?
Turnover is ordinarily very low in our department. However we recently lost our network administrator.
Describe any unfilled positions.
We are looking for a network administrator to supervise our Windows/NT Server network. We are also looking for a Web Master, with Internet and Intranet experience.

continued . . .

Information Systems Personnel Issues
Are any necessary technical skills (such as network support) unavailable within your IT group at this time?
Internet/Intranet and JAVA Experience.
Do you have a plan in place to hire additional personnel to become "self-sufficient," or do you plan to outsource these requirements?
We plan to hire additional staff to support our Intranet and our Internet Web site.   *We may outsource JAVA programming if we cannot locate the right person for this position.*   *We plan to have an Internet Service Provider to host our site during our initial "construction" period.*

Information Systems Effectiveness	**1 (not effective) to 5 (very effective)**	**Comments**
Financial Systems	4	*Our G/L, A/P, A/R and Payroll applications are working well.*
	1	*Our PO system is not automated.*
Manufacturing / Production Systems	3	*We have a project tracking system but it does not help schedule subcontractors*
Distribution Systems	1	*We would like to interface our Order Entry system with the Internet to enable us to accept orders from our European distributor.*

continued . . .

Information Systems Effectiveness	1 (not effective) to 5 (very effective)	Comments
Sales and Marketing Systems	3	We get most of the reports that we need. But we would like to use the Internet to support our regional sales people, and to enable us to market our training products to Fortune companies.
DRS and Administrative Systems	5	Our office runs well. We have very few problems and our GA expenses are low.
Messaging and Communications	3	Every employee has a PC for e-mail. We want to set up an Internet mail gateway.
EDI systems	1	We will need to implement EDI to support our European distributor next year.
Local Area Network	4	Our system performance is good, but we are supporting too many different platforms.
Wide Area Network	1	We want to use the Internet to support remote information access.
Internet Connectivity	1	We plan on implementing another Intranet server next quarter to support our production team's work.

continued . . .

Information Systems Effectiveness	1 (not effective) to 5 (very effective)	Comments
End-User Training	4	Our users are comfortable with our information systems. However they would like to be able to use Internet e-mail.
End-User Help Desk	4	We can usually respond to users within 15 minutes.
Training and Documentation	4	We have our vendors' documentation - and have created a User Procedures guide for our network administrators.
New Application Development	3	We are using Visual Basic to generate custom reports, and to help Human Resources manage employee records.
Compensation / Motivation	4	Our IT staff is well compensated, and is looking forward to migrating to network computing.
Audit and Security	3	We back up all data on tapes, and rotate tapes for off-site storage. We are investigating remote server backup options.
Other		

IT OPERATIONS OVERVIEW

The easiest way to reduce IT support costs is to provide every system user with the tools, including training, system documentation and help desk support, that they need to get their job done effectively.

If IT training and systems documentation are provided in an ineffective manner, users will waste a great deal of the IT department's support personnel's time. This approach lowers users' productivity, and will ultimately impact the productivity of everyone in the organization that depends on their output.

IT PROCEDURE HANDBOOK

The most effective way to document mission-critical tasks is to create a Procedure Handbook.

Preparation of a User/Procedures Handbook
1.   Define your objectives for your Procedures Handbook.
2.   Plan to document each mission-critical application and/or every service that your IT department provides.
3.   Collect information on tasks, procedures and policies.
4.   Flow chart tasks and procedures as needed.
5.   Create a draft of the handbook "for comment."
6.   Have handbook reviewed for accuracy and completion by supervisory personnel.
7.   Implement revisions and create final draft of handbook.
8.   Have handbook reviewed and approved by relevant managers.
9.   Print and distribute handbook and/or publish handbook online.
10. Conduct orientation / training session with users.
11. Update handbook as needed.

EXAMPLE PROCEDURE

The following is an example of how an IT procedure can be documented. It is a simple, straightforward way of enumerating the tasks involved in all IT procedures.

Accounts Payable/Month End Procedure

PURPOSE/OBJECTIVE

This procedure automatically posts open AP transactions to the General Ledger.

PERSONNEL

This procedure may only be performed by an authorized AP Clerk, or the CFO.

SCHEDULE

Perform this procedure at the close of business, on the last business day of each calendar month.

TASKS/STEPS

1. Run Accounts Payable reports.
    See Accounts Payable Reporting Procedure for a list of reports that must be run each month.

2. Select "Post to General Ledger" on the Accounts Payable module's Maintenance Options menu. The system will automatically post all transactions into the correct General Ledger accounts.

3. Print two copies of the Aging Payables Report. Send one copy of this report to Bill Henderson, and the other copy to Larry Gates.

PROBLEMS/ERROR MESSAGES

*   If you get Error Message 1162, make sure that all system users have signed off of Accounts Payable, and then rerun the procedure.

*   If you get Error Message 2211, ask the System Administrator to help you repair the damaged index files.

IMPACT ON OTHER APPLICATIONS OR SYSTEMS

The Accounts Payable detail file must balance with linked General Ledger accounts.

AUTHORIZATION / APPROVAL / EFFECTIVE DATE

This procedure may be modified by the CFO or the IT Manager. (4/97)

Documentation	• **Complete** • **Accurate** • **Clear** • **Concise**	• **Easy-to-Use** • **Easy-to-Reference** • **Easy-to-Maintain**
Vendor Documentation (installation, implementation, and operating instructions)	Excellent coverage of basic system operations	Vendor has not updated its documentation since we installed our system Documentation files cannot be updated to support our modifications
Example: Microsoft Office	Adequate Excellent telephone support is available	Good user feedback
Example: General Accounting	No on-line documentation	Need system integrator's aid to help us interface our custom applications
Example: Documentation Control System	Good documentation	Very easy support
IT Policy Procedures Manuals	Out of date	Must be redone
Accounting Procedures Manuals	Incomplete	Users are responsible for creating their own procedures guide
System Administration Documentation	Network administration documentation is incomplete	Every network administrator goes to 3 weeks of training

continued . . .

Documentation	• Complete • Accurate • Clear • Concise	• Easy-to-Use • Easy-to-Reference • Easy-to-Maintain
	We do not have a user reference for our new backup software	
System Development Documentation	Programmers can use system documentation	Outside training as needed
Data Center Documentation	We have an IT Policy manual which describes all of our procedures	This needs to be updated to reflect new hardware and server procedures
Special Event Documentation	Rely on our IT Manager	
Emergency Documentation	Rely on our IT Manager	
Help Desk	Interrupt driven	Need additional personnel
Vendor's Telephone Support	Support is on a yearly subscription	Varies
On-line Training / Tutorial	User supplied	Varies
User Documentation (Procedures)	We have Procedure Guides for all accounting personnel	Needs to be updated
Video Training	Learning Microsoft Office	Good user feedback
Classroom Training	Classes are scheduled once a month after work hours	Need to contract with an outside training company

continued . . .

Documentation	• **Complete** • **Accurate** • **Clear** • **Concise**	• **Easy-to-Use** • **Easy-to-Reference** • **Easy-to-Maintain**
Member User Groups	Seattle Training Companies Computer User Group	Peer support, information about security issues
Member On-line SIGs	Use CompuServe SIGs	Helpful with hardware issues
Subscription Help Services	Microsoft's Premium Support Plan	Adequate
Other		

ATTITUDES, PRACTICES, AND PROCEDURES

A review of your client's documentation will usually reveal specific products or procedures that are not supported with written documentation, and that may put your client's organization at risk, if trained personnel are unavailable to complete mission-critical tasks.

For example, Client-Centered™ Training does not have adequate documentation for emergency procedures or for the modifications that it has made to its mission-critical accounting applications.

Technical Support	Issues
How much time do users spend resolving technical problems?	Average turnaround is 1 day
How much time do users spend in information systems training classes?	All personnel receive one full day of computer training when they are hired Some personnel receive additional training
What is the IT department's average response time?	Average response time is 60 minutes
When was the last training class scheduled?	Last month

continued . . .

Technical Support	Issues
Was a make-up class scheduled?	No
Was a follow-up review class scheduled?	No
Were personnel tested to ensure skills transfer?	No
Who is responsible for monitoring user satisfaction?	Department Managers - but they have been too busy to manage this
Do you publish a user satisfaction survey?	No
Survey results:	

ATTITUDES, PRACTICES, AND PROCEDURES

If Client-Centered™ Training provided additional IT training for new hires, it could improve user productivity and reduce support costs.

Most system users become unproductive until their technical problems are resolved. By decreasing the IT department's (help desk) response time for technical support, you can directly impact individual productivity.

IT SCHEDULING AND PROCEDURES

Well-organized IT departments run more efficiently, have higher system reliability, less system down time, and ultimately provide a lower cost for their services.

Data Center Scheduling	Issues
System Performance	Overall system performance is good to very good. We have only received complaints when our network was down for software upgrades, hardware maintenance, and power outages.

continued . . .

Data Center Scheduling	**Issues**
Capacity Requirements Planning	We are considering upgrading our LAN from Ethernet to Fast Ethernet to support development of multimedia materials.
Network Management	We use standard SNMP based tools. We are evaluating an upgrade to RMON.
Equipment Over-utilization	Some of our laser printers are run beyond their standard duty cycles; however we have not experienced any equipment failures yet.
Equipment Under-utilization	We are not concerned about under-utilization.
Load Balancing / Managing	We are planning to install Ethernet switches to create subnets which will help us manage network bandwidth and improve throughput for our multimedia development team.
Data Entry Bottlenecks	We would like to implement electronic forms-based procedures in HR and several other departments—this is an ideal Intranet application. We need a document management system to help us manage our production department, and manage file revisions and deletions.
Database Update	Individual users are responsible for all database updates Accounting tables are updated by a subscription service
Database Backup	We back up our main database files each day
Network Mapping	Every user has an account on our system - we plan to provide remote access next quarter

continued . . .

Data Center Scheduling	Issues
Resource Management	We do not have a formal Resource Management program in place
Scheduling non-computer Resources	We use sign-out sheets for PC projection systems and other department resources
SMP Utilization	We are using our server's system management utility to monitor CPU utilization
Memory Utilization	Falling memory prices have enabled us to upgrade our system performance
Security Audit	Yes, see Security Worksheet
Security Update Program	Yes
Does a formalized program exist for goal setting and objectives as a basis for scheduling tasks?	Yes
Does senior management review the IT departments goals?	Yes
Does senior management discuss IT priorities with the IT group?	Yes
Do senior IT personnel join inter-departmental meetings to stay abreast of developments in other functional areas of the organization?	No
Are senior IT personnel aware of goals and objectives of other departmental managers?	No
Are IT services reviewed periodically by departmental managers?	No
Is the IT manager responsible for scheduling system modifications?	Yes
Are users required to forecast their requirements?	Yes
Has a capacity requirements model been developed to establish a baseline for system usage?	We are working on pulling together this information with our network management and administration tools

continued . . .

Data Center Scheduling	Issues
Is a capacity requirements baseline used by department managers to forecast future system requirements and utilization?	Sometimes - for example when new personnel are hired, we try to anticipate their hardware and network requirements
Is there a plan in place to handle temporary increases in system utilization?	No - but we are considering upgrading our network with Ethernet switches to improve performance
Are system utilization levels (IT requirements forecasting process) directly tied to IT budgets for equipment and system support personnel?	Annual budgets for hardware and network resources are tied to our headcount
Has an analysis been done to establish peripheral capacity?	No - we have not had any problem meeting user demand
Are peripheral resources (printers, etc.) adequate to support user requirements?	Generally - but we need better color output capability. We are evaluating high-speed color document printers to support our marketing group.
Other	

MISSION-CRITICAL SYSTEMS

Depending on your client's business, one or more information systems may be critical to support day-to-day operations. In most businesses, for example, order entry is a mission-critical application.

Modifying or replacing mission-critical applications is inherently risky. But while the adage "don't fix it if it isn't broken" is a good heuristic for most business processes, IT managers must continually reevaluate the viability of their legacy systems as new technologies emerge.

You may, for example, need to advise your client to replace its order entry system, if the potential for competitive advantage from implementing a new technology, such as network computing, outweighs the risks inherent in migrating its order entry application to support Internet transactions.

Accounting Systems	Automated	Manual
General Ledger	✗	
Order Entry	✗	
Order Tracking		✗
EDI		✗
Invoicing	✗	
Inventory (BOM)		✗
Accounts Payable	✗	
Accounts Receivable	✗	
Purchase Order		✗
Job Costing	–	–
Sales Tracking / Reports	✗	
Customer Database	✗	
Human Resources IT	✗	✗
Payroll	✗	
Desktop Publishing	✗	✗
Manufacturing Systems	–	–
Production Control		✗
Shop Floor Control	–	–
MRP	–	–
CRP	–	–
Scheduling		✗
Time and Billing		✗
Data Collection Systems		✗
Other		

Office Systems
Is your telephone system adequate for your business needs? Yes *Our telephone consultant has done a good job.*
Are your accounting systems adequate for your needs? No *Our basic accounting system is adequate. However, we need to implement additional applications such as production control, scheduling, time billing for our consulting group, purchase order tracking and EDI when we begin to work with our European distributor.*
Do you use an electronic mail system? Yes Is it adequate for your business needs? *No, we need an Internet mail gateway to communicate with our customers.*
Do you use the Internet for electronic messaging? Not yet
Do you maintain your own Web server? Not yet
Do you plan to make any significant changes to your office systems within the next twelve months? Yes *We plan to implement a purchase order system next quarter, and additional applications as resources become available.* *We plan to implement an Intranet server to support our training material production group.* *We also plan to host a Web site on the Internet.*

DOCUMENTING IT SYSTEMS

Documentation which describes the interface between specific business processes and IT systems is extremely important because it enables IT managers to visualize how their systems support specific business objectives.

One way to document complex IT systems is to create work flow diagrams which include the names and primary functions of each application and system component, and then to map each workflow to the users and processes which are supported.

When different IT managers document an IT system, they will invariably create diagrams which are very different from one another. Fortunately this is not critical, because the primary purpose of creating these diagrams is to help management visualize how its IT systems "map" to specific business processes and objectives. If that goal is met, the specific documentation techniques employed are irrelevant.

When you document your client's IT systems, you should feel free to create your own style-guide to represent processes and system components on your diagrams. However, be consistent and avoid too much detail to help you communicate as clearly as possible. In most real world situations, useful IT systems documentation spans many pages. The simplified diagram below describes a basic A/R process, related IT systems and key personnel.[7]

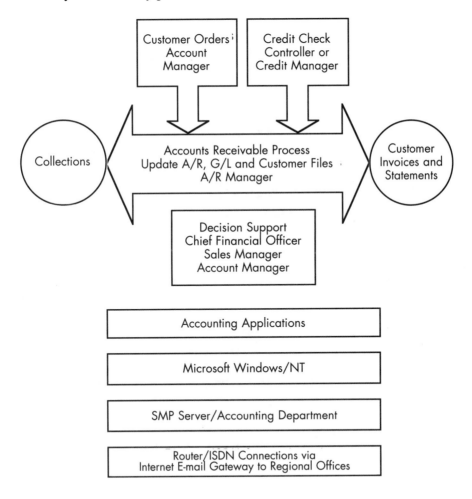

---

[7]These diagrams were created with Visio Version 4.0.

The next diagram presents a document-centric, workflow A/R application.

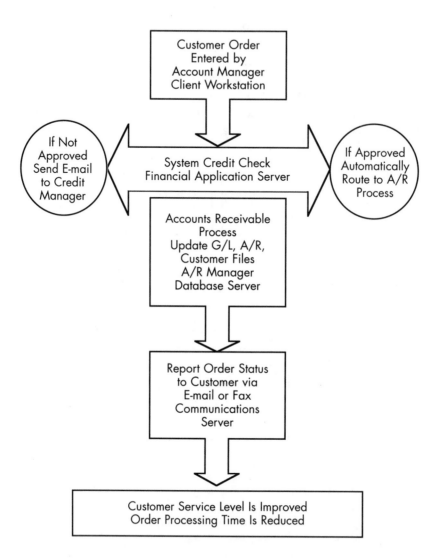

In Chapter 8 we provide a step-by-step methodology for evaluating user requirements, and for evaluating the pros and cons of reengineering specific business processes.

DEFENDING THE IT DEPARTMENT

IT managers are usually comfortable identifying several areas of their department that can use improvement, or that need to be reengineered. However, in most cases, a comprehensive IT audit will reveal many additional areas that need attention. Depending on an IT manager's personality and sense of job security, discussing these deficiencies may cause him or her to become defensive.

Generally, if you are professional, candid, and avoid making judgments or personalizing your comments, you will find that IT managers will attempt to cooperate with you, and will try to enlist your help in resolving their department's problems.

System Bottlenecks	Primary Concerns
System Administration	We need to hire a new Network Administrator. We want to look into remote server backup options.
System Management	We want to install an SNMP network management system that can help us identify LAN bottlenecks and improve our network's performance.
Timeliness of Receiving Data	Departmental level reporting is good, but executive level summary reports do not provide the information our managers need to track open projects. We would like to implement a project management system that provides drill-down capabilities.

continued . . .

System Bottlenecks	Primary Concerns
Accuracy of Data (Data Integrity)	Our accounting systems update accounts in real time. We would like to have a decision support tool which enables us to monitor our strategic financial ratios on demand.
Data Access / Reporting Capabilities	We have good data access to our financial systems from our local workstations. We need to support remote user access. We do not do a good job of tracking and controlling development projects.
Flexibility	We are using Visual Basic to customize each user's interface. We believe that this will help us improve each user's productivity.
System Response Time	Our system response time is beginning to suffer because of multimedia document creation. We plan to upgrade our LAN with Ethernet switches to fix this problem.
System Reliability	Our systems have been remarkably reliable. We have experienced virtually no down time - except for scheduled system upgrades - since we migrated to Windows/NT Server eighteen months ago. We do not have a disaster plan in place.
Security	We need to improve system security. Currently we use passwords to limit access to our network; however, file level security has not been implemented, and user security policies, such as periodically changing passwords, are not enforced.

continued . . .

System Bottlenecks	Primary Concerns
Systems Integration (Interoperability)	We do not have a good plan to integrate our current document management system with our Intranet servers. We are exploring the advantages of migrating all internal documents to HTML format. We have standardized on Visual Basic for Applications to enable us to share data between our office productivity applications and our order entry and scheduling systems.
Extensibility (Expansion Capabilities)	We want to standardize on Windows Open Services Architecture APIs, Windows/NT, Intel PCs, and standard Internet protocols to help ensure the highest level of interoperability between our systems.
Rapid Application Development (RAD) Capabilities	We plan to provide internal training and support for anyone that wants to use Visual Basic for Applications to create custom programs. Our developers are using Microsoft's Visual Basic, SQL Server and C++, and are learning JAVA.
Support (Suppliers)	We have a contract for on-site support for all of our hardware and network systems. We are satisfied with our support provider.
Service (Suppliers)	We have one-year service agreements in place with Microsoft and our Accounting Software supplier. We would like to contract with an outside programming service or a senior consultant to help us with Visual Basic application development.

continued . . .

System Bottlenecks	Primary Concerns
Service (Internal Personnel)	We do not have any one assigned to handle our Help Desk. This function is handled on an "as available" basis.
Is a plan in place to resolve these outstanding problems?	We are working on many different plans to resolve these outstanding issues. However, we have not been able to create a master IT strategy that ties our plans together.
Can any of these problems be resolved by outside suppliers?	We cannot identify and evaluate suppliers until we have a better understanding of our own capabilities and limitations.

Decision Support Capabilities	Information Access and Reporting
• Business Unit	Our data warehouse provides summary information which can be accessed by our PC-based OLAP and data mining applications.
• Customer Class	We can extract views of our data by customer class. (Seminar / Consulting / Major Account)
• Geography	We can generate reports on our East and West regions; however, we cannot generate reports on international sales. We are concerned that our current accounting systems cannot support multiple currencies.

continued . . .

Decision Support Capabilities	Information Access and Reporting
• Product Line	We can generate reports on a product line basis; however, we cannot get detailed information on individual products.
• Product	We can only generate information on individual product lines. However consulting revenues can be analyzed by customer, and type of project.
• Sales Group / Representative	We can generate sales reports for each account manager.
• Other	
• Summarize Sales Trends	We use Microsoft Excel's pivot tables and charting features to help us interpret our reports. However, we do not have any direct link into our accounting system to help us visualize sales trends.
• Overall Satisfaction With Decision Support Capabilities	Although our system is limited in certain areas, it is extremely easy to use, and can be augmented using custom Excel reports. Our managers are satisfied enough with our current DSS capabilities to resist learning a new application.

RESOURCE MANAGEMENT

IT departments should have a system in place to keep track of all hardware, software, and other IT assets. Automated resource management programs are available from Computer Associates and other suppliers.

Hardware Inventory
Company's (Asset) Inventory Number: Sales PC - 15
Primary User: West Coast Sales Manager
Office Number: 1405
Product Use: Desktop Workstation
Description / Notes: Pentium Pro PC
Manufacturer Intel Clone Computers Address: 3490 Highway 99 City, State, Zip: Bellevue, WA 98101 Sales Contact: Angel Duncan is our Account Manager Date of Purchase: July 24, 1996 Purchase Cost: $4,380
Maintenance Information Serial Number: KCFT36548-PCEW Passwords and/or User ID: gnome Maintenance Contact: National Service on Call Service Phone: (800) 555-1212 Date of Service Agreement: July 24, 1996 - 1999
Configuration Information CPU Type and Speed: Pentium Pro 200 MHz Memory Configuration: 32 MB Graphics Adapter (manufacturer / model number): Good VRAM Board Monitor (manufacturer / model number / capacity): Best Vision Math or Other Coprocessors: Hard Disk (manufacturer / model number / capacity): OEM 2.5GB Optical Disk (manufacturer / model number / capacity): Best DVD Backup Storage Unit (manufacturer / model number / capacity): 230 MB Network Card (manufacturer / model number / capacity): NDIS OEM Network Settings: (port / interrupt / other): IRQ 5 Modem: USA ISDN

continued . . .

Hardware Inventory
Printer (manufacturer / model number): Network Laser Printer SCSI and Other Devices: Scanner Pro on COM1 port Other:
Maintenance Notes Machine serviced by Tom Brown on February 12, 1997. No known problems.
Interoperability Issues Video card is incompatible with Windows/NT 3.0, but works with Windows/NT 4.0.

Software Inventory
Company's (Asset) Inventory Number: Sales OS-PC-15
Product: Windows/NT Server
Description (Operating Environment / Special Modules / Other) Windows/NT Version 4.0 Operating System
Primary User: Departmental Mail Server
Office Number: 1405
Product Use: Non-dedicated mail server and workstation
User's Experience Level: System Administrator
Manufacturer: Microsoft Corporation Address: 1 Microsoft Way City, State, Zip: Redmond, WA 98052 Phone: (206) 555-1212 Sales Contact: Alan Lawrence Date of Purchase: July, 1996 Purchase Cost: $1,485.00
Maintenance Information Product Serial Number: MSFT-123-45-67890 User ID: Bquiet "gnome"

continued . . .

Software Inventory
Maintenance Agreement Number: MSFT-SW-09876
Contact: Fix-It Now, Inc.
Maintenance Phone: 555-1212
Date of Support Agreement: August, 1996 - 1998
Internet Support Address: Windows Help Desk - Scott or Robin
Original Version Installed: July, 1996
Current Version: 4.0
License Restrictions: One copy / one server
User Modifications: Symantec's Network Administration Utilities and H-P OpenView
Network User Counter: N/A
Interoperability Information Works with NDIS card Use Windows/NT TCP/IP stack
Outstanding Problems Incompatible with 16-bit version of our Mapping software.

Asset Inventory
Company's Asset / Inventory Number: UPS - 19
Primary User / Location: Primary Mail Server
Office / Plant Number: Office 1405
Asset Use: Backup power supply for primary mail server.
Description / Notes: Provides 2 hours of battery backup.
Manufacturer: ABC Power Contact Information: Donald Volt Address: 321 Power Drive City, State, Zip: Redmond, WA 98052 Sales Contact: Computer Place Date of Purchase: July, 1996 Purchase Cost: $350.00

continued . . .

Asset Inventory
Supplier's Part / Serial Number: *UPS-350*
Maintenance Contact: *None*
Service Phone
Date of Service Agreement
Maintenance Notes: *Replace when LED test lamp does not light up.*

APPLICATION REVIEW PROCESS

Most IT departments have a formal application review process to ensure that new applications are working properly before they are rolled out to support critical business operations.

Planned Changes to Information Systems[8]
1. *We plan to automate our purchase order system next quarter.*
2. *We plan to install an Intranet server to support our training material production group.*
3. *We plan to host a Web site on the Internet to help us market our products.*

continued . . .

---

[8] This information may be covered in earlier IT Audit Worksheets.

Planned Changes to Information Systems[8]
4. We plan to implement Fast Ethernet switches to support our multimedia production team.
5. We plan to implement a company-wide security policy.

Auditor's Recommendations *Note:* **This worksheet provides an executive summary of the auditor's recommendations. It is not intended to replace a complete Information Technology Audit Report.**
1. Client-Centered Training is planning to use the Internet to help it market its training products and consulting services. C-CT should consider implementing an Internet gateway on its LAN to support communications with its subcontractors, business partners and customers. C-CT should also consider migrating its existing network and workgroup applications to Internet protocols. This would enable it to leverage its multimedia production capabilities.
2. Billing and A/R costs are in line with industry expectations. There would be very little advantage in outsourcing these applications.
3. After C-CT has implemented its Intranet server, it should consider implementing a Purchase Order system which supports EDI.
4. C-CT's IT personnel's skills are in line with expectations. However, the IT department needs to recruit technical personnel that have experience developing and maintaining commercial Internet Web sites.
5. C-CT needs to develop IT budgets which reflect its planned expansion into Europe, Asia and South America, and its intent to use the Internet to develop an alternate sales and product support channel. We recommend a complete IT Budget review. The IT Audit process is covered in Chapter 7.

WHAT'S COMING UP?

In the next chapter, you will learn how to identify the technologies which are most likely to impact your organization; how to anticipate technology "break points" which may impact your business; and how you can evaluate the potential benefits and "hidden" risks of becoming an early technology adopter.

CHAPTER 6

EVALUATING
NEW TECHNOLOGIES

The computer industry invests over a billion dollars each year marketing leading edge technologies. But many companies fail to realize the benefits that have sold them on implementing these technologies.

Deloitte & Touche, for example, surveyed 221 executives to determine whether or not they were satisfied with their client-server accounting systems. Results were rather surprising. Only 9% of the executives described their system as "world class"; 85% of the executives said their systems "fell short" of their expectations.[9] Fortunately, there are many criteria that you can use to help you evaluate the risks of implementing new technologies.

THE CURMUDGEON'S RULE

The author's "Curmudgeon's Rule" states that IT managers should never assume that a system they are evaluating provides any functionality that is not explicitly specified and documented. Furthermore, they should not assume that every specified or documented functionality is available or works properly, until it is tested in their own shop. In other words, "what you see is what you get."

The Curmudgeon's Rule is supported by several observations:

1. The IT landscape is littered with obsolete concepts, products, technologies and standards.

---

[9] 57% of the executives wanted better reporting tools; 48% wanted better ad hoc analysis; 67% said that they would implement the technology in the next two years; and 71% reported that they had already downsized their IT staffs in the past two years.

Despite these problems, the client-server accounting market is expected to grow from $922 million in 1994 to over $3 billion by 1999.

2. Technological innovation is often synonymous with instability and incompatibility.

3. Promises from vendors may or may not ever be fulfilled and new products may or may not ever be delivered.

4. The availability of pre-release software on the Internet does not necessarily mean that a useable product will ever be installed in a real production environment.

5. The most popular and useful products are often in beta-development or on backorder for so long that less desirable products must be installed and implemented.

In addition to the ramifications of the Curmudgeon's Rule, you must also understand the "Get A Grip" Observation—that business success does not necessarily depend on anything an IT department does or doesn't do.

Adopting an emerging technology, such as network computing, may enable your company to gain a competitive advantage against less automated competitors. But business success hinges on a number of elements. An effective advertising campaign, an introduction to an important client, or access to inexpensive financing, are just a few of the countless factors that may help a business succeed.

> IT managers are rarely given the resources (time, personnel and equipment) that they need to evaluate different technologies before being asked to render opinions and make decisions about those technologies that may impact their organization's future success.

HARBINGERS OF IT SUCCESS

Fortunately there are a number of heuristics that you can use to help you evaluate the potential impact of emerging technologies on your business.

- *The market for new technologies is driven primarily by market demand, not technological innovation. Businesses are interested in learning about technological innovations, but they buy solutions that work.*

  Products based on leading-edge technologies do not do well in the market if they fail to provide affordable, easy-to-install, implement and maintain solutions which meet their customers' needs.

  For example, many companies are exploring ways to leverage the Internet with commercial Web sites; however, most companies today are implementing private Intranets, partitioned from the Internet by "firewalls," because they do not feel that the Internet is mature enough to provide the data integrity, security, and reliability that they need to manage business applications.

- *By analyzing mission-critical business processes, you may identify specific tasks which can be "reengineered" to improve your business operations.*

  Many companies have implemented Web sites on the Internet to help them provide customer support.

- *Reengineering these tasks may provide an opportunity for your business to gain a competitive advantage in your market.*

  Maintaining an Internet server as an alternative to staffing additional telephone support personnel can help a business lower its operating expenses. These savings can be passed along to customers, and may provide an advantage over competitors who have not established an Internet presence.

- *Successful installations are a better predictor of the potential value and maturity of an emerging technology than the amount of money a supplier has spent on development, or marketing hype.*

  In most cases, the best spokesperson for an emerging technology is an early adopter who has successfully implemented the technology, and who has realized some advantage.

- *As a new technology matures, the companies which supply and support the technology will consolidate.*

  The Internet market has experienced a tremendous amount of consolidation as company after company has dropped out of its market, been acquired, or has "reinvented" its Internet strategy.

- *As a market matures, de facto standards emerge and products become "commoditized." The more similar products are, the easier they are to second source, and the more competitive suppliers must be to win market share.*

  Twelve months ago, over a dozen companies were competing in the Internet browser software market. Today, Microsoft and Netscape produce similar Internet browsers which control over 95% of the market.[10]

---

[10] Internet browser software enables a computer that is connected to the Internet to access World Wide Web sites. In the future, this functionality will be included in most computers' operating systems.

- *As new technologies become easier to install and implement, more users will adopt them.*

  The Internet did not become widely used until Internet Service Providers distributed easy-to-use "point and click" software and easy-to-implement, inexpensive Internet e-mail accounts.

- *As new technologies become less expensive, more users will adopt them.*

  AT&T started a "price war" by announcing it would provide unlimited dial-up Internet access for $19.95 per month. CompuServe, another Internet service provider, responded almost immediately by announcing it would provide a similar service for $17.95 per month.

  Some analysts predict that Internet access may eventually be bundled into the cost of standard telephone service by competing telephone services providers. However, it is unclear at this time how extended Internet usage will impact telephone tariffs.

- *As technologies mature, suppliers will continue to add value to maintain their customer base.*

  Two years ago, Internet service providers supplied a connection to the Internet and support for electronic mail. Today, ISPs are adding value by providing bundled Internet explorers, and access to proprietary multimedia information and Bulletin Board Systems (BBSs) that enable users to dialog about specific topics of interest.

  In the future, the Internet will provide additional services, such as real-time audio and videoconferencing, and media distribution.

- *Evaluate every technology "opportunity" in the overall context of your business plan.*

  The Internet might enable you to reach geographically distant customers more cost effectively than your current sales and marketing programs.

- *Stay focused on achieving your primary business objectives.*

  Evaluate short-term benefits to determine whether the new technology is worth its "opportunity" cost.

TECHNOLOGICAL INNOVATION

- *Does the technology enable new mission-critical solutions?*

  Emerging technologies that enable companies to reengineer mission-critical business processes are the most likely to impact a business's fundamental business model.

- *Does the technology substantially lower the cost of computing or communications?*

  As emerging technologies lower the cost of automation, companies must reevaluate their fundamental cost structure to determine whether they can justify current staffing levels, and whether they must reengineer existing business processes.

- *Does the technology impact production or manufacturing?*

  If a technology will impact production or manufacturing it is critical to get those personnel involved with the evaluation process. Experienced production personnel can often identify shortcomings of emerging technologies that would not be apparent to IT personnel.

- *Does the technology impact research and development?*

  Technical specialists want to work with the very latest development tools. However, the risk factors associated with migrating to new development tools can be very great.

  Many companies bring in outside consultants (the devil's advocate) to evaluate internal IT recommendations to change any systems level tools, such as programming languages, databases or operating systems, that have been used to develop and deploy mission-critical systems.

- *What areas of your business will be impacted by technology?*

  The LOB (line of business) managers that will be impacted by a technology should be consulted before scheduling any technology demonstrations or starting any pilot programs.

- *Will the technology fundamentally change your business model?*

  If you believe that an emerging technology will change your fundamental business model, you should consider the implications with your board of directors as soon as possible.

- *Will the technology impact your businesses' competitiveness?*

  Emerging technologies often provide a "window of opportunity" to early technology implementers. Use the heuristics outlined later in this chapter to evaluate the pros and cons of being an early technology adopter.

- *Will the technology enable your company to reduce operating expenses, increase profitability, or enter new markets?*

  The only time a business should incur the risk of adopting emerging technology is when it is convinced that doing so will enable it to improve its bottom line or address new business opportunities.

MARKET ACCEPTANCE

- *Is it intuitively obvious how and why the technology will benefit potential customers?*

  Technologies which succeed in the market offer a compelling "story" based on providing straightforward solutions to fundamental business problems. Technologies which cannot be easily explained are usually soon forgotten.

- *Are two or more technologies competing for market share or market dominance?*

  The best technology does not always win against better marketed alternative technologies. If you have to "bet" on technological savvy or marketing acumen, it is usually safest to put your money on Madison Avenue.

- *Will acceptance of an emerging technology be impacted by one or more industry standards?*

  Standards organizations can impede the implementation of new technologies for years. If the success of a new technology depends on establishing an industry standard, make sure that the companies which are marketing the technology have the financial resources and commitment to drive market acceptance.

- *Is acceptance of the technology contingent on future technical advances or "breakthroughs"?*

  Innovation is not predictable. A new technology may be developed in a month, a year or may never "germinate." As a rule, technologies that rely on future technical advances should only be adopted if your company can afford to write off the project as a research expense.

- *Is adoption of the technology contingent on the developer being able to finance the launch of products based on the technology? Is the technology being backed by a financially secure "deep pocket"?*

  The more money that is invested in a new technology, the more likely it is to succeed. However, financial strength alone cannot ensure success. IBM and Apple, for example, teamed up to develop a new object-oriented operating system called Taligent. After several years of effort, and millions of dollars of investment, the Taligent group was shut down without ever releasing a product.

- *Is the technology proprietary?*

  Most companies today are choosing products based on "open" standards. Products based on proprietary technologies are unlikely to be successful in the market unless they provide substantial price or performance improvements over existing technologies.

- *Will there be multiple sources of supply?*

  Technologies which are licensed to multiple suppliers are usually more successful in the market than technologies which are only supported by one vendor. This is why semiconductor manufacturers and software developers that develop new products often "cross-license" their technology to competitors.

- *Are any major companies supporting (purchasing and implementing) the technology?*

  The broader the base of support that a technology has, the more likely it is that products based on the technology will continue to be supported and enhanced.

- *Have any of your competitors installed or implemented the technology?*

  If your competitor has implemented an emerging technology, and has improved its cost structure, you may need to do the same to remain competitive in your market. However, companies that adopt new technologies tend to "sell" the benefits that they are supposed to realize before they actually do. You should perform your own due diligence before assuming that your competitor's new system is providing the benefits claimed.

- *When do you believe the technology will become widely adopted in your market segment or industry?*

  Tracking the implementation (life) cycle of an emerging technology will help you determine the best time to bring the technology into your organization. As technologies become more widely adopted, implementation costs usually decline, and implementation risks are generally reduced by a better support infrastructure.

IMPLEMENTATION ISSUES

- *Does the technology obsolete your currently installed mission-critical systems?*

  Replacing systems which handle mission-critical applications is riskier than implementing information systems which handle new tasks.

- *Can the technology be implemented in phases?*

  Implementing new technology in phases reduces your organization's risk factors.

- *Can your business afford to evaluate the technology in-house?*

  Testing a new technology in-house in a limited pilot program, before "rolling out" the technology throughout your organization, is one of the best ways to reduce your organization's risk factors.

COMPATIBILITY

Standards have emerged for many IT products. For example, about 80% of LANs support the Ethernet network protocol, and about 90% of PCs use a version of Microsoft's Windows operating system. Purchasing products that are compatible with industry standards can help your organization reduce procurement, installation, implementation and maintenance costs over the life of the product or system.

Advantages of Purchasing Products That Are Compatible with De Facto Standards
• Supported by leading hardware and software suppliers, and system integrators
• Products are tested by suppliers and/or independent testing services for compatibility with de facto standards, so users have less chance of encountering technical problems
• Products from "third-party" suppliers are available to enhance product usability
• Knowledgeable support personnel and training resources are readily available
• Good chance of having product supported in the future
• Good chance of suppliers supporting earlier releases of product in future product releases
• User groups are established
• Reduce procurement, installation, implementation and maintenance costs over the life of the product/system

INTEROPERABILITY

Every time two hardware or software components are connected, they must pass information back and forth, facilitated by an interface that both components understand. The interface between two software components is called an API or Application Programming Interface; the interface between a hardware component and a software component is called a device driver.

The interfaces between different components can be very complex. For example, a complex multi-level interoperability model has been created to describe each component of the interface between two software applications which are sharing information across a network. This model, which is called the Open Systems Interconnection protocol, specifies exactly what signals must be transmitted between two software applications to begin a "peer-to-peer" transmission, address each data packet, secure the data that is being transmitted and control every aspect of the communication process.

Standardizing on specific interfaces can drive the adoption of new technologies by enabling suppliers to use standard components to lower their development, manufacturing and marketing costs. But it is very difficult for standards organizations to keep up with the rapid pace of technological innovation. Companies which are developing new products must often define their own "de facto" standards to support their new products.

If the companies that develop new products are successful in the market, their "de facto" standards often form the basis for subsequent industry wide "de jure" standards. De jure standards are created and maintained by independent review boards, such as the International Standards Organization (ISO).

If companies that are marketing new products are unable to build significant demand for products based on their de facto standards, their competitors may collaborate to develop an "open" standard, which levels the playing field for their own products.

- *Developing IT Standards*

  Microsoft and Intel have formed an alliance to promote industry wide PC standards for a wide range of multimedia and system management interfaces. If their effort is successful, these initiatives will be adopted by leading PC hardware and software suppliers, and will resolve many interoperability issues. However, IT departments which have older (legacy) PC systems will have to cope with incompatible systems.

  For example, Visioneer is a leader in the rapidly growing personal scanner market. Visioneer's device drivers, which interface their scanners to PCs, are compatible with PCs that use Intel Pentium processors, but are incompatible with older 80486-based PCs that have been upgraded with Intel's Pentium OverDrive™ Processors. Organizations that have upgraded some of their older PCs with these processors cannot standardize on Visioneer's scanner for all of their legacy PCs.

- *Implementing IT Standards*

  Many IT standards are implemented before products based on those standards are brought to market. However, many technologies are evolving so quickly that standards organizations are unable to publish their recommendations before products based on those emerging technologies are released into the market.

  For example, Proxim, Inc. has recently announced a new 1.6 Mbit/sec. specification for wireless LANs called RangeLAN2. Proxim announced this specification 5 years after the IEEE 802.11 standards committee began working on a wireless LAN standard.

  Proxim approached IEEE two years ago about adopting RangeLAN2 as a basis for its specification, but was turned down because the IEEE group believed that it could develop a better standard. However at this point, the IEEE group has yet to publish a specification.

According to Proxim, the entire wireless LAN industry has suffered because there has been no standard, and claims that this standards "vacuum" has led to proprietary vertical applications being developed.

Proxim believes that its new standard will be adopted and licensed by other wireless LAN suppliers, and that it will ultimately enable customers to mix and match access points and client hardware from many different suppliers.

If Proxim is successful at promulgating its standard, manufacturing volumes should go up, which will in turn drive wireless LAN prices down. As prices decline, the market for wireless LANs should grow rapidly.

Estimated U.S. Wireless LAN Market
Installed Base in 1000s of Users
Source: Proxim

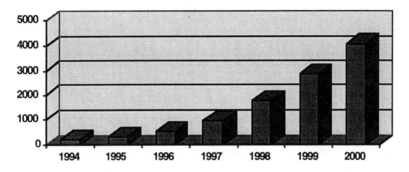

- *Supporting IT Standards*

  IT standards are meaningless unless they have a wide base of industry support, and are enhanced frequently enough to support new innovations.

  For example, LDAP the Lightweight Directory Access Protocol—is a good example of how emerging technologies, such as network computing, drive the computer industry to develop and implement new standards that support the development, marketing, adoption and deployment of new business solutions.

  Virtually every major networking systems supplier, including AT&T, Banyan Systems, Inc., Digital Equipment, Hewlett-Packard, IBM, Microsoft Corporation, Netscape Communications, and Novell have announced support for LDAP.

  However, LDAP is a subset of the X.500 network directory services protocol and only provides basic directory services. LDAP will need to be extended to support ancillary functions such as network management services.

If competing networking system suppliers develop open, rather than proprietary, extensions to LDAP, the protocol will open the door to true interoperability between disparate networking resources. But if proprietary extensions are marketed, the LDAP standard will fail to solve the problem of incompatible network directory services.

Purchasing IT products that support standard interfaces is the easiest way to ensure that products from different companies will work together properly. But rapid technological innovation, and resulting product incompatibilities, have made it extremely difficult for IT professionals in larger organizations to configure interoperable, enterprise-wide solutions.

EASE OF USE

The most effective way to ensure adoption of emerging technologies is to make them as easy to install, implement, manage and support as possible. For example, PC manufacturers are very concerned that emerging Internet "appliances" (network computers) will be easier to use than PCs and that they will ultimately replace PCs in many businesses.

Intel's Desktop Management Initiative (DMI), Microsoft's Plug and Play specifications, and the Universal Serial Bus (USB) standard, which make PCs easier to use and manage, are the opening salvos in a campaign by Microsoft, Intel and other industry leaders to help ensure that PCs do not lose market share to less expensive network computers.

PERSONNEL ISSUES

IT, like all other businesses, is ultimately a "people" business. If your IT staff is receptive to a new technology, and has the experience to install, implement and maintain that technology, your implementation risks will be much lower than if your personnel are resistant to deploying the new technology.

- *Do your personnel want to adopt the new technology?*

  The best way to ensure successful adoption of a new technology is to obtain the support of senior management, and of the IT personnel who will be directly responsible for implementation and support.

- *Do you have personnel on staff that can support the new technology?*

  Having trained technical personnel on staff helps mitigate any problems that may arise during installation and implementation of new technologies.

If no personnel on your staff can support the new technology, you will have several options.

1. *Train existing personnel*

   In most cases, training your existing personnel is the best way to ensure the integrity and viability of your information systems.

2. *Hire new personnel*

   In some situations, you will need to hire technical specialists, such as database experts that have training and experience working with a specific RDBMS.

3. *Outsource the task*

   Another option is to retain an outside service bureau or IT consulting group to manage some or all of your IT systems.

4. *Partner with a company that has the resources to implement the technology*

   Another way to lower your risk is to form a partnership with a technology-oriented company, and then rely on its IT personnel to provide information systems management and support.

5. *Delay implementation until the technology is easier or less expensive to implement*

   If you believe that a new technology will be of benefit to your organization, but are concerned about implementation risks or poor return on investment, your best course of action may be to delay adoption until you are convinced that the benefits of implementing the new technology more than outweigh your risk factors.

   Emerging technologies become "commoditized" over time. This process generally leads to improved ease of use, interoperability and performance, greater access to technical resources, and less risk of encountering insurmountable technical problems.

DEVELOPING A TECHNOLOGY EVALUATION PROGRAM

Implementing a technology evaluation program is the most effective way to stay abreast of how and when emerging technologies may impact your organization's competitiveness or fundamentally change your industry's business model.

A technology evaluation program can also help your organization predict when products based on new technologies will impact your business operations. For example, the declining cost of personal desktop scanners and PC fax modems has enabled many PC users to migrate from standalone fax machines to fax modem—equipped PCs.

The program should be staffed by at least one senior technical specialist responsible for presenting a report to senior management at quarterly IT update meetings. At this meeting, the technical specialist can discuss emerging technologies and products which may enable the organization to reduce costs, improve profitability or address new business opportunities. Also to be discussed are the costs and risk factors of adopting those technologies, and when appropriate, an action plan for evaluating those technologies in-house.

SOFTWARE REVIEW PROCESS

Most IT departments use a formal software review process to determine whether or not a new application is ready to go online. It is generally comprised of four steps:

- **Requirements Review**

  A requirements review is generally performed after a user requirements analysis and after a preliminary functional specification has been drafted. This review is designed to clarify communications and incorrect assumptions, and identify any missing user requirements. The output of the requirements review is approval to complete an application design review.

- **Application Design Review**

  An application design review provides an objective analysis of the project development (programming) plan.

  Depending on the application, and the experience level of the programming staff, it may be necessary to perform a complete top-down review of the application development process, as well as an evaluation of specific program functions.

  In some cases, the design review will also focus on the development environment, rapid application development tools, and database technologies that are being used to support application development and deployment. The output of the application design review is approval of the application design.

- **Code Review**

  Application code should be consistent with the IT department's programming standards, and should meet all of the functional requirements specified in the application's user requirements analysis and program design specifications. The output of the code review is acceptance of the team's programming approach and methodology.

- *Testing Process*

Software testing often begins with individual software components (business objects) which are linked together to support specific application requirements.

To ensure that the testing process is sufficient to detect all program errors, it should include a review of all test data and programming cases (possible processing scenarios).

Most software testing in object-oriented programming environments is automated, to test as many programming events as possible. So it is imperative that the application developer's testing methodology be "bullet-proof." The final output of the testing process is acceptance of the application for implementation.

Software Review Process
Project: Commercial Web Server / EDI Implementation
Date/Time: August 15, 1997
Description of Project: Implement Commercial Web Server and interface it to our RealWorld Visual Accounting Order Entry and Billing System. Then, make the Commerce Server work with our EDI Package.
Project Development Manager: Robert Thomas
Development Team Members Alan Brooks, Peter Jones, Judy Whitney
Documentation Manager: Phyllis Smith
Testing / Quality Assurance Manager: Linda Johnson

Review Results:
  • ACCEPT
  • ACCEPT WITH SPECIFIED MODIFICATIONS
  • REPROGRAM - MAKE SPECIFIED CHANGES
  • REDESIGN - MAKE SPECIFIED CHANGES
  • REVIEW INCOMPLETE - STATE REASONS

continued . . .

Software Review Process
Application Review Notes Installed Windows/NT and Internet Commerce Server. These are fully functional. The EDI system needs to be modified to work with our Order Entry System.
Review by: Alan Daniel Date: August 14, 1997
Received by Development Manager: Date: August 16, 1997 Comments: We may need to call in an outside consultant that is familiar with our EDI package to ensure that we can have our system operational within three weeks.

COMPLETING SOFTWARE PROJECTS

A recent Standish Group survey found that 31% of software development projects are canceled before coding is completed; and that on average only 16% of software projects are completed on time and on budget. In larger companies, only 9% of software projects are completed on time and on budget.

Software projects that reach deployment in larger companies contain only 42% of the originally proposed features and functions; but in smaller companies, 78% of software projects reach deployment with at least 74% of their original features and functions.[11]

SOFTWARE MAINTENANCE

Most business software applications require ongoing maintenance which is comprised of programming fixes, revisions and modifications.

- *Program Fixes*

    Correct programming errors, operating deficiencies, errors, bugs, incompatibilities with other (interoperable) systems.

---

[11] Source: Standish Group survey reported by Adam McCauley in *Open Computing* March 1995.

- *Program Revisions*

  Revise program to support changes in business processes or government legislation.

- *Modifications*

  Revise or "modify" program to support new or enhanced functionality.

Many IT departments have new hires and entry-level programming personnel work on software maintenance tasks. This gives them an opportunity to learn their code base, become familiar with common programming errors, and become acquainted with the organization's programming methodology and departmental procedures.

SOFTWARE UPGRADE ISSUES

It is common for software companies to release new versions of their products every six to nine months, and for hardware manufacturers to revise their products and "extend" industry standards as often as needed to beat off competitors and emerging competitive technologies.

Despite companies' insatiable desire to generate revenues from software updates and hardware upgrades, many IT managers are reluctant to implement them. Upgrades are expensive, are often less stable than more mature product releases, and are often incompatible with one or more other hardware systems or software applications that are supposed to work together.

IT System Upgrade Issues
• Management Planning
• Changes to Departmental Infrastructure
• Testing Lab
• Hardware Upgrades
• Software Upgrades
• Incompatible Software (replace or fix)
• Installation
• Asset Inventory
• Train End-Users

continued . . .

IT System Upgrade Issues
• Train PC Technicians
• Train LAN / WAN Support Personnel
• Train Developers / Analysts
• Other

NEW APPLICATION REVIEW PROCESS

Formalizing the new application review process will help prevent unexpected problems.

New Application Review Process
• Meets User Specification
• Meets Internal Programming Standards
• Procedural Logic
• Information Sharing or Transfer
• Performance on Target Systems
• Supports Internal Standards for Business Objects
• Coordinated with Database Administrator (DBA)
• Coordinated with Network Administrator
• Coordinated with Security Officer
• Maintainability
• Backup Procedures
• Error Messages
• Test Data
• Test Procedures
• Test for Standard Error Conditions
• Test for All Conditions
• Manual Backup Procedure
• Test in Production Environment

continued . . .

New Application Review Process
• Programmer's Documentation
• User Application Guide
• Online Documentation
• Online Help Files
• Online Tutorial
• Coordinated with IT Manager
• Departmental Roll-out Scheduled

SERVICE / SUPPORT

You can use the Vendor Support Questionnaire to help you understand and evaluate your supplier's sales and support policies *before* making any purchase decisions.

Vendor Sales and Support Questionnaire	Services Provided
Equipment supplied:	Fast Ethernet Switching Hubs Internet Server Color Laser Printers Microsoft Windows/NT Server
Did supplier manufacture or OEM this equipment?	No
Do you charge separately for:	
• Options / Accessories	Yes
• Delivery	Yes
• Installation	No
• Maintenance	Yes
• Support	Yes
• Training	Yes

continued . . .

Vendor Sales and Support Questionnaire	Services Provided
Do you rent or lease this equipment? Describe terms:	We use Don't-Go-Way Leasing Company to finance all IT purchases. Terms for this sale are $15,000 down, and $600 per month for 60 months. There is a (10%) purchase option at the end of the lease. You may add additional equipment to the lease with credit approval.
Do you provide discounts for: • Quantity orders? • Bundled deals? • Promotional packages? • Beta or trial user sites?	N/A We will provide 16 hours of installation support with the Ethernet switch. We pass through any current promotions on Server products. N/A
Do you have cover shipping costs? Do you guarantee shipping times?	Yes We will advise you of any delays.
Do you accept or broker trade-ins? If so, how does your trade-in program work?	No.
Do you sell reconditioned or demonstration equipment? What warranties are available on this equipment?	Yes, when it is available from suppliers. Varies All accessories and supplies are sold as is.
What services are included with installation? • Facility Planning • Who is responsible for installation planning?	Yes Our customers
• Machine Replacement	We will provide backup machines if they are available.

continued . . .

Vendor Sales and Support Questionnaire	Services Provided
• Machine Checkout	We test system before delivery.
• Software System Generation	Included with software installation.
Do installation charges include any necessary travel or lodging expenses?	No
Do you perform a comprehensive system check during installation? Do you perform installation optimization or system diagnostics?	Yes We use our manufacturer's diagnostic tools.
If you do not provide warranty service, maintenance and system support, who does?	We provide repair on all servers. Network equipment is supported by LAN AHOY, Inc.
What coverage is provided by your Service Agreement? For example, "telephone support 7day X 24 hour service" or "8:00AM to 5:30PM PST Monday through Friday."	7X24 telephone service. Same day on-site service.
How are parts and labor covered? For example, "1 year parts, 90 days labor warranty" or "all parts except printer suppliers."	Parts and service are covered by manufacturer's warranty. Minimum coverage is 1 year on parts and 3 years on labor. Extended service agreements are available on most systems.
Cost for Service Agreement Payment Terms	$345 per month for proposed service contract.
Period of Service Agreement	Contracts are available for 1 to 4 years after expiration of manufacturer's warranty.
Is your Service Agreement transferable?	Software agreements may only be transferred with original hardware.
Is local support available?	Yes

continued . . .

Vendor Sales and Support Questionnaire	Services Provided
What are the qualifications of supplier's service personnel?	*Better LAN Support has 3 Microsoft CP LAN specialists.*
Is a minimum configuration a prerequisite for maintenance?	*No*
Does installing components that have not been supplied by the vendor void warranty or Service Agreements?	*No, unless there is a physical incompatibility.*
Do you provide telephone support?	*Yes, 7 X 24 support is available*
Do you provide remote diagnostics?	*Yes, we can use RMON to support remote system diagnostics and adjustment.*
Do you pay shipping on parts?	*No, this is handled by each supplier.*
Do you have a formal training program for your support personnel?	*Yes. We send all technical personnel to our supplier's advanced training programs.*
When, where and for how many hours / days is training offered?	*We offer network system training on site on an as needed basis.*
How much does your support training program cost?	*Most services are $105 per hour.*

OUTSOURCING INFORMATION SYSTEMS

Many Fortune companies are outsourcing some or all of the information processing systems to companies, such as IBM and Digital, that have the hardware, software and systems integration experience necessary to implement and maintain reliable, secure computing and communications resources. Worldwide information technology outsourcing is expected to grow 25% per year.[12]

If your company is considering this, you will need to carefully analyze costs and benefits. In most cases, outsourcing can be cost effective for companies that have information systems budgets of over $2 million per year.

---

[12] Source: G2 Research, Mountain View, California, (Network World, May 20, 1996, pg. 19)

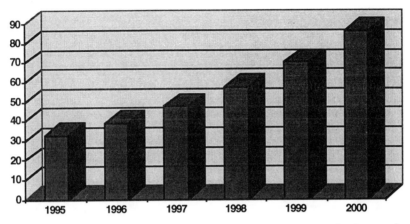

Worldwide Information Technology
Outsourcing in $Billions

Source: Gz Research

Companies should only adopt new technologies when they are convinced that their potential for increasing productivity, reducing operating expenses, or generating new business outweighs the costs and risks of implementing the new technology.

CHAPTER 7

SECURITY, ORGANIZATION, AND DOCUMENTATION

SECURITY

There are five issues that IT managers should consider before adopting a security strategy: accountability, auditability, integrity, usability and cost.

- *Accountability*

  In larger organizations one individual is usually responsible for overall system security; IT security officer is typically a mid-level management position in the IT department. However, every system user must be held accountable for protecting the organization's information resources. Revealing passwords or providing information that could potentially enable a hacker to breach the organization's IT system is tantamount to sabotage or theft. In all cases, access to system resources should be limited to users whose jobs require access.

- *Auditability*

  Maintaining system security requires auditability. The IT security manager should be aware of when authorized system users are accessing information, what information is being accessed or modified, and when and how unauthorized attempts at system access are being made.

  Most IT managers maintain access, violation and modification logs to monitor system usage.

  - *Access logs*—record who attempted to log on.

  - *Violation logs*—record who attempted to violate file/system security.

  - *Modification logs*—record who modified system files.

    In addition to these logs, revised versions of modified files can be stored to maintain a complete audit trail of system usage.

- *Integrity*

  IT security systems are not perfect. Virtually any system can be defeated or circumvented if an attacker can access and modify the system's (operating) systems level files. Different systems level applications have varying degrees of protection against unauthorized access. For example, Microsoft Windows NT's file system is more secure than that of Windows 95. However, in most cases, system attack can only be deterred by implementing a comprehensive security policy.

  For example, systems that support remote connections can be set up to automatically call-back the remote user's modem to help authenticate the location that the user is calling from. This does not completely protect a system from attack, but it makes it more difficult for a hacker to impersonate an authorized user.

  Similarly, an organization which has implemented an Internet gateway can install a firewall which scans each incoming message packet to determine whether the user (sender) is authorized to access and modify any of its system's program or data files. A more precise way to determine the boundaries of system integrity is to describe a "security kernel" that is defined by three attributes: completeness, isolation and correctness.

  - *Completeness*—the security kernel monitors all access to all system objects.

  - *Isolation*—the security kernel is protected from modification or interference from any external program or method.

  - *Correctness*—the security kernel performs its security functions properly, and does not interoperate with any other systems, or perform any other functions.

- *Usability*

  IT system security should be flexible enough to define and grant access to system information and resources *as needed* with a minimum of IT management overhead. If security concerns dominate, additional machine overhead and user time will be needed to maintain the security systems. If concerns about system security are minimal, such as in a home office environment, senior management may choose to implement minimal security measures.

  In any case, information is of little value if it cannot be accessed easily. So organizations must balance their users' concerns about ease of information access with their need to achieve a high level of overall system security.

  The most effective way to ensure that users will comply with established security procedures is to make those procedures as simple as possible. For example, requiring users to change their passwords every week is counterproductive in most business environments. However, in financial institutions, this may be necessary, particularly when any personnel with system administration privileges leave the organization.

* *Cost*

   Computer security requires a commitment from senior management to invest the resources necessary to protect their corporate information systems. The security measures and the related costs of implementing and maintaining system security should reflect the value of the information that is being protected.

   For example, financial institutions, at great risk of external attack, encrypt data files and transmissions, limit physical access to their systems, monitor network traffic, install state-of-the-art firewalls, implement redundant data storage and backup, and manage all of their security procedures very carefully. Businesses which are less likely to attract the attention of hackers and cyber-criminals typically make a much smaller investment in securing their IT systems.

ENCRYPTING DATA FILES AND MESSAGES

One of the most effective ways to secure data is to encrypt it. The Data Encryption Standard (DES) published by the National Bureau of Standards is the most widely adopted "symmetric" cryptosystem. A symmetric cryptosystem uses the same "key" to encode and decode information. The larger the number of digits in the key, the more difficult it is to break the code, hence the more secure the encoded information.

Asymmetric (public key) cryptosystems rely on two keys, a public key and a private key. Messages are encrypted with the recipient's public key, and can be decoded only by the recipient using a unique, secret private key. Therefore, an unauthorized user who breaches the sending computer's operating system's security and gains access to the sender's encryption key file will not be able to read any data or messages that have been encrypted with the recipient's public encryption key unless the recipient's secret private key is also accessed. The U.S. government currently restricts export of the most powerful data encryption tools. However, legislation to remove these restrictions is being considered at this time.

CIRCUMVENTING SYSTEM SECURITY

No commercial systems are absolutely safe from attack. How easily an IT system's security can be circumvented is a function of several factors:

- physical security (physical/plant level)

- user awareness and compliance (user level)

- operating system environment[13] (systems software and application level)

- Local Area Network system environment (network operating system and application level)

- Wide Area Network environment (implemented at the "firewall" and outside of the organization on public and private virtual networks)

FIREWALLS

A firewall can be implemented as a screened host or subnet firewall, or an application proxy server firewall. A screened host firewall controls access to a single host computer by means of a router operating at the network level. A screened subnet firewall controls access to an entire network by means of a router operating at the network level.

Network level firewalls tend to be very fast and transparent to users because they operate by screening data packets for valid (IP) address blocks. Incorrectly addressed packets cannot pass through the firewall.

Application proxy server firewalls check every byte of information that is sent to them, and decide whether or not to pass data packets not only on the basis of their (IP) address blocks, but on their content. They can, for example, be programmed to pass specific types of information, such as electronic mail, thereby protecting the network against any attacks except those targeted to electronic mail services.

Firewall Security Issues

- Make sure that your IT security and network access policies are consistent with your overall business objectives and that they make sense from a technical viewpoint.

- After identifying and prioritizing your security objectives, with a comprehensive needs analysis and risk assessment, you can put together a checklist of what should be permitted, monitored and denied.

continued . . .

[13] For example, C2 level security requires user authentication, auditing, discretionary file access, resource isolation and network auditing. More robust B2 level security requires mandatory file access controls which are not set by users.

Firewall Security Issues

You may, for example, deny users all but the most critical business services, or you may allow users to access additional services, such as FTP or Real Audio, to provide metered or audited Internet access.

Some companies restrict access to specific Internet sites, such as ESPN's sports news site or Playboy's Web site; other companies choose to trust their employees to make intelligent decisions about how to spend their time at work, and do not limit Internet access.

- Maintain centralized administration and monitoring authority.

- Make careful decisions about what level of monitoring and report auditing you want in your firewall.

  You may need to consult a security expert to help you balance your desire to monitor everything with the practical reality of being overwhelmed with audit data.

- When you implement a firewall, be sure to close off all other in-bound access points, such as remote communications servers, to your network. Otherwise you may be "hacked" through a back door.

- Segment your mission-critical and most sensitive information from Internet access to reduce your exposure to attack.

- Depending on your security requirements, you may choose to configure your existing routers to filter incoming traffic via IP addresses; use an application-level proxy toolkit to build your own firewall, or purchase a firewall from an independent software vendor (ISV).

- Finally, determine the life-cycle cost of your firewall. Evaluate your costs based on both acquisition costs and continuing costs.

  Firewalls are constantly subjected to security breaches and firewall suppliers are continually updating their products. To optimize your firewall, and maintain maximum protection from attack, you may need to install and support patches and configuration changes on a weekly basis.

  Implementing a robust firewall can take up to several man months of time, and may require four to eight hours per week for ongoing system management and reconfiguration.

COMPUTER VIRUSES

Computer viruses are destructive programs that can infect a computer and damage applications and data files. Most computer viruses can "replicate" themselves and be transmitted as hidden files or program components, from one computer to another.

It is hard to understand why a programmer would be driven to create a computer virus. Perhaps it is because of insecurity, and creating a destructive virus provides some ego reward. In any event, virus protection software is available to protect computer systems from infection, and to disinfect those already infected. But so far, the programmers who create virus are staying one step ahead of those who create virus protection utilities.

Most computer viruses are transmitted along with information that is being downloaded from the Internet. But once in awhile, a virus is distributed by an unaware software supplier on a standard software installation or upgrade disks.

Many IT departments restrict program installation to qualified technicians, and prohibit users from downloading any programs or data files from the Internet, or from any other external source. However, there are many types of viruses, such as macro viruses which infect document files, and complex polymorphic viruses.

When a user executes a program infected with a polymorphic virus, the virus takes over control of the computer and un-encrypts the main body of the virus. The complete virus can then take over control of the user's computer. Polymorphic viruses encrypt themselves using a different scheme each time they infect a computer, so that they can change their code sequence or "signature." This makes them extremely difficult to detect, and capable of breaching all but the strictest security measures.

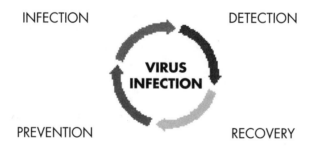

INFECTION   DETECTION

VIRUS
INFECTION

PREVENTION   RECOVERY

Virus Infection Cycle	Factor
Source	• Reused and borrowed disks • Programs downloaded from BBSs, online services and the Internet • Opened, pirated, software • Preformatted disks • Software from reputable software developers that has been infected
Infection	• Boot from infected disk • Reboot with infected disk left in drive • Run infected program
Spread	• Shared disk or infected program • Log on to network
Detection	• Unusual system behavior • Missing files • Disabled programs • Virus detected by virus protection software
Recovery	• Reinstall programs from master disks • Repair files with antivirus software • Restore files from uninfected backup
Prevention	• Rescan all files to find virus • Scan all disks to find virus • Discard infected disks or backups that may be infected to increase virus protection • Restrict access to untested data sources • Schedule automatic (background) virus scanning • Inoculate uninfected files with virus checker such as Symantec's AntiVirus™

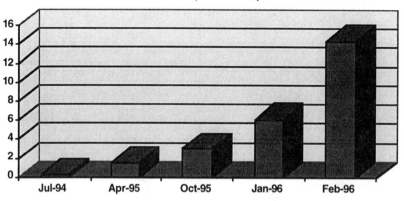

Number of Virus Encounters per 1,000 PCs per Month
Source: National Computer Security Association

DISASTER RECOVERY

Every IT department should have a comprehensive disaster recovery plan. The plan should include procedures for recovery from both natural disasters and premeditated, malicious attack on critical information systems.

Common IT problems such as electrical outages should have recovery procedures posted in a "special situations" procedure handbook. For example, storms often cause electrical outages. IT personnel should have step-by-step instructions on how to maintain critical systems using backup power facilities, and how to recover any transactions which were not completed during the power outage.[14]

Example Power Outage Procedure

1. Call all departments to advise them of the power outage, and to advise them to use their
   paper backup forms for all new business.

2. Make sure the Uninterruptable Power Supply (UPS) on the network file server is functioning correctly.

3. Perform a (daily) *complete system backup* on a *new* removable high-capacity disk if the UPS has enough power reserve.

4. Check the transaction error log.

5. Verify that all transactions that have been logged in the Error File have been rolled back.

6. Call all department heads, and send out an e-mail notification to all system users when the power outage is over and the system is operational.

---

[14] Most relational databases automatically "roll-back" incomplete transactions to maintain the integrity of their data files.

Security Issues	Risk if Not Implemented	Difficulty to Implement Feature	User Involvement Aggravation
Physical Access to Servers	High	Low	None
No Local Storage	Moderate	Low	High
Limit Client Applications	Moderate	Low	Moderate
Internet Firewall	High	High	None
Restrict Remote Access	Moderate	Moderate	Moderate
Virus Protection	High	Low	Low
Password Controls	Low	Moderate	Moderate
File Access Controls	Moderate	Moderate	Moderate
Administration Rights Controls	Moderate	Moderate	Moderate
Dial-up Port Controls (Auto Callback)	Moderate	Moderate	Low
Data Encryption	High	Moderate	High
Activity Log Maintenance	Moderate	Moderate	None
Operating System Security	High	Moderate	None

ORGANIZATION AND MAINTENANCE

IT departments, like other departments in your organization, will be more effective it they are well organized.

Organizational Issues	Outstanding Issues
Are organizational issues delegated to one or more managers?	The IT manager delegates specific tasks to different members of the staff.
Are organizational concerns documented?	We are not aware of any at this time.
Is adequate space available for equipment and personnel?	Yes, we have a small room devoted to our network and application servers.
Is software usage monitored?	Yes, a program on our application server monitors the number of users accessing each application we have installed.
Are hardware systems in good repair?	Yes, all of our equipment is covered by service contracts.
Is all equipment organized and labeled?	It is organized. But our network cables are not labeled properly.
Are all peripherals in good repair?	Yes, all of our equipment is covered by service contracts.
Is surplus equipment stored properly?	We try to dispose of surplus equipment to people on staff, or we donate it to non-profit organizations. We don't let it sit around.
Is documentation available and organized?	Yes
Is all maintenance information available and organized?	System reference materials are stored in the IT office.
Is data storage media organized and indexed?	Yes, each person is responsible for backing up work files. Production personnel keep a log of all current work files. The system administrator backs up the network file server each night. Backup files are indexed online.

continued . . .

Organizational Issues	Outstanding Issues
Are magazines, newspapers, and correspondence organized?	No, we receive too many magazines; many are never read. We are using Internet publications to replace some periodicals.
Are adequate housekeeping services available?	Yes
Are all cabling systems installed properly and maintained?	We have Category 3 wiring installed. We are evaluating the cost and benefit of running Category 5 wire to our desktop.
Are HVAC systems operating properly?	Yes
Is fire equipment operational and recently inspected?	This is handled by our landlord.
Is Human Resources information posted appropriately?	We keep all HR notices on the bulletin board in our lunch room
Is the IT area secured?	We have a ten-digit key pad on the door to our main computer room.
Are all visitors checked-in and given identification badges?	No, but we plan on implementing this security step next month.

DOCUMENTATION

Documentation helps users install, implement, and maintain automated systems. Well designed documentation enables users to solve their own problems and become less reliant on IT support personnel.

> As a rule, the easiest way to lower support costs is to provide and maintain easy-to-understand documentation.

DOCUMENTATION CRITERIA

- *Accuracy*

Documentation must be accurate or it will not be used.

- *Completeness*

  Documentation must provide a reasonable "service level." If it does not answer most questions, users will find other sources for information and support.

- *Clarity*

  Documentation must be clearly written. If it requires "interpretation," users will consult PC power users in their organization, or call IT personnel.

- *Conciseness*

  Verbose documentation is difficult to use and expensive to maintain.

- *Ease of Access*

  Documentation must be easy to access. One of the best ways to provide user documentation is to maintain it online.

- *Ease of Reference*

  Online information must be easy to access, and should have hypertext links (or should include clear and specific references) to related help topics.

- *Ease of Maintenance*

  Documentation should be maintained in parallel with product enhancements and system modifications. If it is not maintained it will soon become incomplete, inaccurate and ultimately worthless.

- *Use of Documentation*

  IT Group should track support usage by department and/or task, to help it justify its IT budget, and to help it evaluate the usefulness of written and online documentation, help desk services, and any other components of its department's IT support infrastructure.

- *Documentation Log*

  A Documentation Log which lists undocumented user problems and other relevant issues can be used to identify recurring problems. It can also be used to help negotiate favorable support contracts with system suppliers. It is hard for suppliers to increase prices on products which have caused problems!

- *Frequently Asked Questions (FAQs)*

  Frequently Asked Questions can be addressed with documentation supplements and training programs.

IT DOCUMENTATION

- *System Procedures Handbook*—Documents all standard procedures.

- *Directory of Resource Personnel*—Documents which internal and third-party resources are available to solve specific user problems

- *Overview of System*—Provides a "top-down" view of IT systems to enable the reader to understand the interface between different systems and applications

- *Workflow Guide*—Describes electronic forms routing and procedures.

- *Descriptions of Individual Tasks / Procedures*—Individual user guides for each application.

- *Data Integrity Issues*—Describe DBMS methodology and schema.

- *Data Security Issues*—Describe security policies.

- *Company Policies and Guidelines*—Describe all employee policies and guidelines (usually maintained by Human Resources department).

- *Documentation Log*—Lists all documentation that is available within the IT department.

- *Log of Vendor Contacts*—Lists contact and phone for all suppliers and support resources.

- *Guide to Help Resources*—User guide which supplies a "road map" to all help resources available online, through internal support personnel, or through external system suppliers or third-party support vendors.

INFORMATION TECHNOLOGY BUDGETS

The budgeting process is used as a management tool for planning and control. To be successful, the budgeting process—like any other business process—must be carefully managed.

The first step is to define the organization's primary information systems requirements. These should reflect both short- and longer-term business objectives. To articulate these requirements, it is important to ensure open debate on current IT services and on new business opportunities that may require new or expanded information systems or support services.

Next, the IT department should develop an operations plan that defines its objectives, and an action plan that describes how and when resources will be allocated to support its users' IT requirements. Last, the action plan should be reviewed by senior management to determine whether the resources required to achieve the IT department's objectives are available, and to verify that low-cost, low-risk solutions are chosen whenever possible.

IT department budgets are typically based on four assumptions:

1. The IT department is a separate cost or profit center. Most corporate IT departments are cost centers.

2. The IT department has budgetary accountability.

3. The IT department has some way of monitoring and charging services to the departments within the organization that it serves.

4. Corporate management includes IT in the budgetary planning process, rather than simply giving the department a quarterly or yearly operating budget.

THE BUDGETING PROCESS

Virtually every IT organization uses one of three budgeting processes: *incremental,* *zero-base* or *baseline* budgeting.

- *Incremental Budgets*

  Incremental budgets are adjusted on the basis of a company's business objectives, such as sales revenues, and on "external" factors, such as inflation.

  Objectives such as corporate sales revenues and head count are often used to assign incremental budgets. For example, if a company's sales increase by 25%, a $200,000 IT budget may be increased (indexed) by $50,000 to support this growth.

  Although it is the most commonly used budgeting process, it is also the least accurate way to anticipate an IT department's requirements. For example, if the example company's sales increase 25%, it may cost far more than $50,000 to replace computer and communication systems that cannot scale to accommodate this growth; and if sales decrease by 25%, it may be impossible to maintain mission-critical systems if the IT department's budgets are decreased by $50,000.

- *Zero-Base Budgeting*

  Zero-base budgeting, pioneered by Texas Instruments Corp., is based on the idea that budgets should reflect the value of specific activities relative to achieving specific business objectives. For example, if one of an organization's objectives is to implement Just-In-Time inventory management, funds may need to be budgeted to install and implement an electronic data interchange system.

  In zero-base budgeting, managers divide their annual budget into small components called "decision packages." Each decision package describes what the manager wants to do, how to do it, alternative approaches that have been considered, how much it will cost, how it will benefit the organization, and what the consequences will be if the proposed budget item is not approved.

  After defining these decision packages, the manager prioritizes the decision packages to reflect the organization's objectives, and sends the budget to senior management for approval. Zero-base budgeting is time-intensive because it requires a great deal of interdepartmental communication and cooperation to identify and prioritize objectives, and to evaluate different approaches to reaching those objectives.

  Line of business managers often have priorities different from IT personnel, and can provide valuable input into IT budget allocations. Companies that do not rely on zero-base budgeting should review their IT department's budget semi-annually to ensure that resources are allocated consistent with their LOB manager's objectives.

- *Baseline Budgeting*

  Baseline budgets rely on fixed or lowest cost budget figures for most budget items, such as long-term equipment leases, and a limited number of decision packages to address specific requirements, such as improving its help desk's response time. It is often used to justify changes in equipment configuration and the acquisition of new systems.

  Baseline budgeting provides a compromise between the accuracy of zero base budgeting, and the ease of implementation of incremental budgeting. Its major limitation is that it assumes that baseline budgets are necessary to achieve a business's objectives. This assumption makes it difficult to identify budget items which could be reduced or eliminated to cut departmental expenses.

Regardless of the process used, the IT department's budget should include several key items:

1. Forecast of expenditures over time.

2. Breakdown for key budget items as described in the Information Systems Budget Worksheet.

3. Explanation of assumptions that were used in formulating the budget, such as number of support personnel, outsourcing specific operations, and inflation estimates.

4. Brief descriptions of all major systems that will be implemented during the budget period.

BUDGETING IT FUNDS

The Business Research Group, in Newton MA, studied the IT spending plans of over 700 medium-sized to large U.S. companies, with an average annual revenue of $1.4 billion. Its survey respondents included IT managers and executives, CIOs, and corporate vice presidents.

BRG found that personnel expenses as a percentage of companies' total IT budgets have fallen from 39% three years ago to 31.3% in 1995. They expect personnel expenses to remain at about 31% over the next few years because most IT departments have reached their staffing goals after downsizing over the past few years.

How U.S. Companies Are Allocating Their 1996 IT Budgets
Source: Business Research Group, Cahners Publishing, Inc.

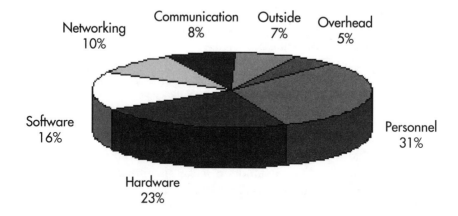

BRG also learned that IT departments have increased spending on outside services from 4.8% three years ago, to over 6.5% in 1995. BRG believes this reflects IT departments' increased reliance on outside consultants, particularly when implementing new technologies such as client/server systems.[15]

Information Technologies Budget Worksheet	Last Year's Budget	This Year's Budget	Percent Change
Salaries, Wages, Other Payroll Expenses	260	290	+12%
Recruitment Expenses	15	15	0
Training, Continuing Education, Travel, Entertainment	20	30	+50%
Operating Supplies	10	10	0
Services	5	5	0
Equipment Depreciation	--	--	--

continued . . .

---

[15] Source: *Datamation*, June 1, 1996

Information Technologies Budget Worksheet	Last Year's Budget	This Year's Budget	Percent Change
Maintenance	40	45	+13%
Hardware Rental/Lease	160	170	+6%
Software	100	90	-10%
Networking	70	115	+64%
Application Development Services	20	30	+50%
Strategic Planning	--	--	--
Building / Office Depreciation or Rent	--	--	--
Utilities	15	15	0
Telephone / Facsimile Charges	110	125	+14%
Communication and Internet Connection Charges	120	130	+8%
Taxes (other than Payroll)	50	60	+20%
Miscellaneous Administrative Expenses Allocated to IT Dept.	50	55	+10%
Outsource to System Integrator	80	60	-25%
Other Expenses	--	--	--
Total Budget Amount			

Before presenting a budget for senior management's approval, the IT manager should be sure that it:

- Clearly identifies the organization's needs that are being addressed.

- Provides an explanation of alternate solutions when relevant.

- Specifies the IT department's recommendations, and explains why the IT department is committed to this course of action.

- Contains a "best estimate" of when the IT department will be able to implement the course of action specified in its budget.

> Managing growth by failure does not make sense; however, in many companies, IT budgets are not increased until corporate growth stresses information systems to the point of "failure."

CONTROLLING COSTS

The budgeting process is also used to help control costs.

In most IT departments the primary expense is for personnel costs, including recruiting, training, wages and benefits, payroll administration, job evaluation and supervision, and union relations.The only way to control these costs is to put procedures in place that manage the hiring process, and to periodically review employees to determine their value to the organization.

Non-personnel costs must also be managed. Most companies implement a four-step cost control procedure.

- *Expense Administration—Approval Procedure*

  Management should implement a purchase approval system for all requisitions over a specified dollar amount. This policy should apply to any requisition, regardless of previously designated budgets.

  In most companies, different levels of management are authorized to approve purchase orders for different dollar amounts.

- *Document Costs*

  Clear, accurate records should provide a clear account of how the IT department has used its resources, including time, money, equipment and facilities. This record should be easily understandable by the organization's controller.

- *Compare Costs to Standard Costs*

  All expenses should be reviewed to determine whether they compare with standard (competitive) costs for similar services, materials or equipment.

  Costs should be reviewed periodically. PC costs in particular, which continue to decline, should be reviewed monthly, or on a per purchase order basis. Other costs, such as long distance line charges, should be reviewed less frequently, perhaps semi-annually.

- *Review Costs*

  Ongoing costs should be reviewed periodically to help control future costs.

  For example, the Controller might review the cost for off-site data storage, or for service bureau charges, to ensure that they are competitive.

PRESENTING YOUR BUDGET

Most departmental budgets are justified three times a year. The first time is during the planning phase, when new business objectives are being evaluated. For example, senior management might be considering the cost to replace its telephone system to support a telemarketing group. The IT department would provide an initial budget estimate to support this opportunity.

The next time is when it is submitted for senior management's approval. At this point, budgets are set based on assumptions about meeting specific business objectives, such as future revenue performance.

The final time budgets must be approved is when funds are actually committed. Most companies implement a senior management approval procedure as a final cost control on major expenditures and hiring decisions that are specified in their business plan.

> The value of the IT budgeting process is largely a function of the degree of trust between senior management and its IT manager. The IT manager who does not believe that the department will be allocated adequate resources to accomplish its objectives will tend to pad the budget, or provide inaccurate or incomplete information, to ensure adequate resources to do its job.
>
> The only way to avoid this type of gamesmanship is to provide an environment that encourages honest communication and makes everyone in the organization feel that they are on the same team.

SELLING YOUR BUDGET

The best way to sell your budget to members of senior management is to convince them that your recommendations provide the lowest cost, lowest risk approach to meeting their business objectives.

- The better you understand senior management's strategic objectives, the easier it will be to position your budget in a way that addresses their primary concerns.

- Be positive, enthusiastic and candid when you present your ideas.

- Do not assume that any items in your budget are self explanatory. Be thoroughly prepared to explain your priorities.

- Stress benefits and solutions, not technologies or product features.

- Be specific about who is doing what.

- If a budget item is discretionary or non-essential be prepared to explain why it is included.

- If budget items have outlived their usefulness, remove them.

- Compare the cost of out-of-house development and deployment of new systems with in-house resources.

- Be prepared to discuss the status of new projects.

- Be prepared to discuss production and efficiency statistics.

- Be prepared to discuss user satisfaction.

- If you are requesting additional personnel, relate this budget request to independence from outside suppliers, better help desk response time, or other tangible benefits that relate to achieving specific business objectives.

ACQUISITION COSTS (THE TIP OF THE ICEBERG)

Hardware and software account for less than 25% of the total cost of implementing an automated system. For example, according to a Gartner Group Study published in *InfoWorld,* upgrading to Microsoft Windows 95, a $50 software upgrade, cost corporations approximately $1,465 per workstation.[16]

Microsoft Win 95 software upgrade $50

Cost of purchasing Win 95 $35

Installation $50

Training IT and end-users $400

Support department review $50

Help desk calls $35

Three application upgrades $300

Cost of purchasing upgrades $35

Upgrade installations $75

End-user training for upgrades $350

Upgrade support costs $50

Help desk upgrade calls $35

Planning costs?

Estimated cost of upgrading 1200 users = $1.5 million

---

[16]Source: Gartner Group Study reported in *InfoWorld* 8/21/95

Estimated Cost of Upgrading Departmental PCs to Windows/NT
Hardware Upgrades $1,000 - 2,000 per system
Software per User $100 - 500
Incompatible Software $75 - 100
Testing Lab $25,000 - 50,000
Management Planning $10,000 - 25,000
Asset Inventory $50 - 150 per desktop
Training End-Users $100 (2 hours)
PC Technicians $1,000 - 3,000 (16 to 20 hours)
Windows/NT Server LAN Support $15,000 - 25,000 (4 to 6 weeks)
Train Developers $40,000
Installation $30 - 60 (2 to 4 hours per desktop)
Changes to Dept. Infrastructure $15,000 - 50,000
Roll-out to End-users $20,000 - 40,000

Hardware	Estimated Cost
• Procurement	
• Installation	
• Integration	
• Maintenance	
• Training	
• Support and Service	
• TOTAL	

Software	Estimated Cost
Procurement	
Installation	
Integration	
Maintenance and Updates	
Training	
Support and Service	
User Group	
TOTAL	

SOFTWARE LICENSING

Most companies' software licenses restrict the use of their software on either a per-user or per-server basis. Software which runs on client workstations is generally licensed on a per-user basis, while that which runs on a server is licensed for use by a specified maximum number of users per-server.

Most applications are used simultaneously by a small percentage of the total number of the users that have access to the application. For example, many people in a company may need to use an application which enables them to create slides or overhead transparencies, but only a few users will need to access the software at the same time.

Many software companies offer concurrent licensing agreements to address this issue. For example, if you have 100 users of a spreadsheet application, but only 20 are ever using the application at the same time, you may be able to purchase a concurrent license for 20 users.

The key to realizing this saving is being able to perform multi-server metering across local- and wide-area networks. The primary advantage of being able to monitor your entire network is that you can monitor simultaneous usage across physical locations and across time zones.

The benefits of application metering allow you to:

- Track compliance with software licenses to avoid costly litigation and penalties.
- Establish enterprise-wide purchasing practices.
- Simplify network management by "normalizing" application storage.
- Monitor software usage and anticipate future demands.

An enterprise-level software metering system should enable real-time license sharing between multiple applications; it should support all network hardware and protocols that you are using, enterprise-wide demand and compliance reporting, and provide the ability to monitor usage of office application suites, such as Microsoft Office. The Concurrent Licenses table illustrates potential cost savings from varying levels of software metering.

Concurrent Licenses	No Metering QTY Copies	No Metering COST $1000's	Department Meter QTY Copies	Department Meter COST $1000	Enterprise Meter QTY Copies	Enterprise Meter COST $1000
Site Meter $10 per Node	0	0	1000	10	1000	10
Office Suite $250.	1000	250	500	125	250	75
Spread Sheet $250	1000	250	500	125	250	75
Database $250	1000	250	250	75	125	40
Project Mgr. $240	1000	250	250	75	125	40
Total Cost in $1000s		1,000		410		240

A new piece of legislation called Article 2B of the Uniform Commercial Code is being considered in Congress. It will define the default terms for licensing software and intellectual property.

If adopted into law, Article 2B will set standards, such as defining whether a software vendor has to guarantee the quality of its software or repair problems with its products after delivering them to its customers.

Article 2B is expected to cover:

- Electronic transactions

- Warranty for quality and definitions of reasonable effort to deliver software as promised

- Liabilities for damages caused by computer viruses

- Intellectual property rights (to underlying information or code)

- Transfer of software licenses

Although Article 2B will set "default" protections, IT managers should continue to protect their organizations' interests with software contracts which address their specific needs.

9

REENGINEERING
IT SYSTEMS

The key to improving business processes is to understand the "who, what, where, when and why" of the process that you are evaluating. Once you fully understand a process, you can analyze each step to determine how to improve productivity and reduce costs.

Many companies employ outside consultants to help them reengineer their operations; however, most companies can analyze their own operations and processes by completing a straightforward Task Analysis.[17]

TASK ANALYSIS

- *Define the Work You Want to Analyze*

  The first step to reengineering a process is to define the work that you want to analyze or restructure.

- *Write a Brief Description of Each Task*

  Pretend that you are an investigative reporter, and get all of the facts. Determine *who* is involved, *what* happens, *when* it happens, *why* it happens, and *how* each task is completed.

---

[17] Adapted from *Computer Solutions for Business* by Doug Dayton, Microsoft Press 1987.

Task Analysis	Example Questions
Who?	• Who is involved? • Are the correct people involved? • Should anyone else be involved?
What?	• What is being done? • What should be done? • Is there a better way to do the work?
Where?	• Where is the work being done? • Why is the work being done there? • Is that the best place to do the work? • Can the work be done somewhere else?
When?	• When is the work done? • Why is the work done at that time? • Is that the best time to do the work? • Is it better to do the work at a different time?
Why?	• Why is the work being done? • Is there any way to eliminate the work? • Should other work be done?
How?	• How is the work being done? • Can the work be done easier, faster, or with fewer resources? • Can these changes be implemented?

If your client is concerned about the effectiveness of its IT systems or its manual business processes in a specific area, you will need to "drill down" on its user requirements to determine whether the IT systems, or any emerging technologies, can help improve their operations.

One way to do this is to create a worksheet that describes the input, processes, and outputs of a specific business activity. You can use a "Story" metaphor to help you understand what the activity is, who is involved, where the activity occurs, why it occurs, how automation can be used to facilitate the process, and the expected impact of your recommended change. The sample "Story" worksheet analyzes a hypothetical order entry activity.

Sample "Story" Worksheet

NAME OF ACTIVITY:

Order Entry and Processing

WHO IS INVOLVED:

- Robert Burns and Tracy Heart - Sales Representatives
- Drew Thomas - Sales Manager
- Tom Brown and Richard Day - Warehouse
- Bill Peters - Warehouse Supervisor
- Mary Pat - Administration
- Al Brown - CFO
- Theresa Sanders - COO

INPUTS TO THE TASK:

Customer's Purchase Orders are entered into the system.

PROCESS - THE ACTUAL TASK:

The customer's credit is checked. If the customer is not over the credit limit or on credit hold, a four-part form is generated.

OUTPUTS FROM THE TASK:

All accounting files are updated.

A customer invoice is printed.

Picking, packing and shipping slips are sent to the warehouse.

---

continued . . .

WHERE DOES IT OCCUR?

The customer order is filled out by a sales representative in the sales department.

The order is sent over to the finance department for a credit check.

If approved, the order is sent to the Accounts Receivable clerk in the Billing Department for invoicing.

The picking slip is sent to the warehouse, completed, signed and sent to the Billing Department where it is compared with the original customer order before a bill is sent out.

The packing slip is sent to the warehouse and is sent to the customer along with the order.

The shipping slip is sent to the warehouse to be given to the freight carrier when the order is shipped.

WHEN DOES IT OCCUR?

Whenever a customer orders merchandise.

WHY IS THE ACTIVITY DONE?

To generate the paperwork that is necessary to deliver merchandise to customers.

To generate the input necessary for the Accounting Department to bill customers accurately for merchandise that is shipped to them.

HOW CAN AUTOMATION IMPROVE PRODUCTIVITY, DECREASE EXPENSES OR PROVIDE NEW BUSINESS OPPORTUNITIES?

A sales representative could use a PC to generate a four-part form when a customer order is received. The form would include the customer invoice and the picking, packing and shipping forms.

The computer could perform credit checking automatically by calling up the customer's file and checking the outstanding balance.

A computerized order-entry system could automatically generate picking slips in a logical sequence to improve the productivity of the pickers in the warehouse.

A computer could update the back-order file immediately when necessary and could automatically print a card to notify the customer of an expected delivery date.

Daily sales journals could be updated immediately for posting to the general ledger, and both the accounts receivable and inventory files could be updated automatically when an order was received and filled.

A computerized order-entry system could generate input for sales analysis reports and sales commission reports.

continued . . .

EXPECTED IMPACT OF AUTOMATION / CHANGE:

Sales personnel will save time because the paperwork involved in order writing will be reduced.

Picking in the warehouse will be faster and more accurate.

Orders will be easier to track.

Paperwork for customer billing will be processed faster.

Collection of receivables will be faster because customer invoices will go out faster.

Accounts receivable and inventory files will be more accurate and up-to-date.

MANAGEMENT APPROVAL FOR SUGGESTED CHANGES OR MODIFICATIONS

Feasibility: I.T. Audit / Consultant

Reasonability: Paul White / Department Manager

Cost Effectiveness: Bart Sanders / Chief Financial Officer

IT Department: William Jones / IT Manager

Final Approval: Theresa Smith / Vice President of Operations

- *Flowchart the Process*

  Flowcharts are a valuable tool for describing different organizational activities. You can use flowcharts in conjunction with your "Story" worksheets to help you visualize each process that you are thinking of automating or reengineering.

  Flowcharts should show the key inputs, the processes needed to accomplish each sub-task, and the outputs of each activity that you are considering automating or reengineering. This is why the "Story" worksheet includes Input, Process and Output subheadings.

  You can use standard IT system flowchart symbols, or just use labeled blocks connected together with lines and arrows to create your flowcharts. The important thing is to make sure that every input, process and output step is represented, and that your diagram is easy to understand.

  Flowcharts are the simplest way to describe how, when, where and why the information that is communicated to different areas of your organization is produced and processed.

- *Review Analysis with Your Client*

  After you have completed your flow chart and your Story worksheet, you should review them with the people involved with the process you are analyzing.

Each person that is involved in a workgroup usually has a slightly different perspective on the work that is being done. Each perspective can help you identify specific steps or tasks that can be improved or eliminated.

Order Entry Flowchart

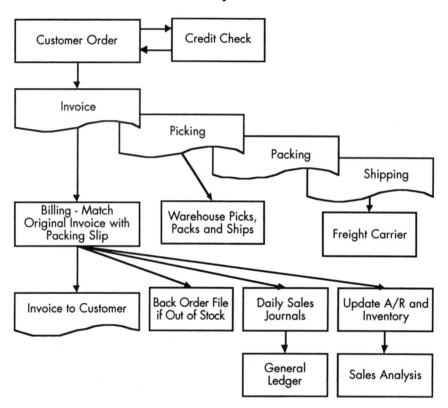

- *Figure Out a Better Solution*

At this point, you can begin analyzing your client's process to determine if any steps can be combined, restructured, or eliminated. This is also a good time to consider the impact of replacing manual information processing and routing steps with automated solutions.

Never assume that a process or a sub-task makes sense because it has been in place for a long time. Look for bottlenecks, redundant data entry steps, audit problems, lack of controls and communication problems.

You should identify the value that is added at each step of the process.

- *Consider Office Automation*

  Implementing automated systems can help an organization increase productivity, decrease operating costs, provide a higher customer service level, and open up new business opportunities

  If, for example, your client routes a paper form through its company, you might be able to reduce its operating costs by routing an electronic form through the company's electronic messaging system.

- *Action Plan*

  After you have completed your task analysis, you can put together an action plan that details your recommendations.

- *Client Approval*

  When your action plan is complete, you should review it with your client. A client involved in your task analysis will usually be proactive about supporting your recommendations. If, however, you have worked autonomously, you should be prepared to do some "internal selling" to convince your client that the changes you are proposing will improve productivity, reduce costs or address new business opportunities.

- *Implement Proposed Changes*

  Before you implement your proposed changes, you should notify all involved personnel of *what* changes are being made, *why* those changes are being implemented, *how* those changes will affect them, *when* those changes are being implemented, and how they can prepare.

  After this notification, it is important to *verify* that every person understands what impact the changes will have on their daily activities.

- *Evaluate Your Changes*

  After your client has implemented your proposed changes, you should determine whether or not they have improved productivity, reduced operating costs, or enabled your client to address new business opportunities.

  If they have resulted in definable benefits, they may become a catalyst for your client to invest additional resources identifying other areas in the organization that can be improved.

  If they have not yielded measurable benefits, you should review your task analysis to determine why they were ineffective, and whether other changes might lead to a more successful outcome.

- *Reasonable Expectations*

  As you embark on your task analysis, try to set your expectations at a reasonable level. Many businesses operate on very small profit margins. The opportunity to increase productivity, even by a modest two or three percent, may make a significant difference in profitability.

- *Implement Rewards*

  In most organizations those individuals that implement new systems are recognized and rewarded, but those responsible for maintaining and improving existing legacy systems are often "invisible" to upper management.

  The hallmark of successful organizations is the ability to continually refine and improve their operations. To accomplish this objective, it is important to recognize and reward the personnel that are involved with task analysis and reprocess engineering.

PROJECT PLANNING

Traditional project planning and management is based on a multiple step process:

1. *Inception / Initial Project Concept*—Gain management approval for feasibility study and systems analysis.

   - Identify organization's need
   - Define strategic objectives
   - Assign project to a project manager
   - Staff project planning group as needed
   - Identify special planning concerns, such as security, confidentiality, etc.
   - Obtain approval (budget) for feasibility study, user requirements analysis and systems analysis

2. *Feasibility study*—Explore potential impact of reengineering business processes and implementing new information systems.

3. *User requirements analysis*—Identify user requirements.

4. *Systems analysis*—Evaluate technologies which can meet user requirements.

5. *Review project status*—Review project status and obtain approval (budget) to develop prototype application.

6. *Project design*—Select technologies which meet user requirements.

7. *Prototyping*—Use RAD tools to develop prototype for user and operations management's evaluation.

8. *Review prototype*—Review prototype with users to finalize design specification.

9. *Final project approval*—Review project status to obtain final project approval (budget).

10. *Specifications*—Develop a detailed project / programming specification.

11. *Programming / Development*—Engineer / develop application.

12. *Testing*—Test application with user data in a simulated production environment.

13. *Documentation*—Create systems level and user level documentation.

14. *Conversion*—Convert data from installed system.

15. *Installation / Implementation*—Cut over to new application.

16. *Integration*—Interface new application with existing applications.

17. *Application review*—Work with users to evaluate success of new application.

18. *Maintenance*—Support users, maintain system, prepare new user requirements specification for future update release.

PROJECT MANAGEMENT ISSUES

- *Small Teams*

  The complexity of project management increases exponentially with the size of the project.

  The more developers working together on a project, the more time will be spent managing and coordinating their efforts, and the greater the chance that one or more team members will produce output that is incompatible with the work other team members are doing.

  In other words, management "overhead" increases as the number of team members increases. At some point, production will actually decrease as additional team members are added.

  Many IT managers assign personnel to development projects on the basis of how many of their developers are not currently working on other "high priority" or "interesting" projects. This approach keeps everyone busy, but it is very inefficient.

A more logical approach to staffing projects is to break the project into sub-tasks that can be more precisely defined, and then to document the sub-tasks well enough for individual team members to work as productively as possible.

Many IT managers deploy their development resources in two or more teams—each working on different parts or phases of a large IT project. Breaking the development process into phases is also a good way to monitor performance, and to motivate and reward "competing" team members.

- *Quick Delivery*

  Different IT managers use different heuristics to help them predict when the completion date of a project will become a "random" event.

  Software development projects which are expected to take over six months to complete, typically take at least 50% to 100% more time than is originally planned.

  Some managers routinely double the development time estimates that technical personnel forecast. Unfortunately, this overly conservative approach is of little value in predicting the completion time (and budgeting) for large development projects.

- *When Is an IT Project Complete?*

  When a programmer or systems developer demonstrates "working code," there may still be weeks, months or in some cases years of additional development work, testing, and integration before the "beta-code" is ready to be implemented in a production environment.

  All IT project development schedules should include milestones for testing, integration, testing, more testing and implementation.

- *Restrict User Involvement*

  It is very important to have user input to help define business processes and system functionality during the requirements analysis phase of an IT project. However, once development has begun, users should let their system developers make system design decisions.

  Micro-managing developers, or making ongoing changes ("feature creep") to the user requirements specification, virtually guarantees that a project will be delayed or derailed.

- *Staged Releases*

  Users often don't know what they want their systems to do until they actually use their system in a "live" production environment. It is often advantageous to specify staged "less than complete functionality" system releases to ensure that large projects stay on schedule, and to help avoid "feature creep."

In many situations, users ask for a "flexible" system, because they haven't taken the time to understand and articulate what they want their system to do.

- *Use High Productivity RAD Tools*

  Many companies are migrating their application development to visual, object-oriented Rapid Application Development (RAD) tools such as Microsoft's Visual Basic to improve their developer's productivity. However, most companies still use procedural development tools such as FORTRAN, COBOL and C to maintain their "legacy" information systems.

- *Define and Use Simple User Interfaces*

  Text-based (3270 terminal style) interfaces are "out." Graphical user interfaces (like Windows) are "cool." Some programmers waste a tremendous amount of time designing artistic rather than utilitarian user interfaces. Whenever possible, you should encourage "elegant simplicity."

- *Source Code Control and Management*

  Use Source Code Control Systems to help manage large development projects.

- *Project Scheduling and Management*

  Use project scheduling and management tools to help manage and control your development personnel.

Systems Analysis Personnel Issues
1. Identify system users and department managers
2. Identify key decision makers in the user environment
3. Identify and verify user's needs
4. Identify and verify user's concerns
5. Identify and verify user's performance expectations
6. Document user's perception of, and problems with the current system
7. Evaluate user's skill level and identify training requirements
8. Draft user requirements specification

continued . . .

Systems Analysis Personnel Issues
9. Will the system replace any personnel?
10. Have personnel moves, adds and changes been coordinated with Human Resources and Facilities Management?
11. Has user training been scheduled and coordinated with affected personnel?

Systems Analysis System Issues
1. Identify and resolve all system interfaces.
2. Identify and specify any special system features or capabilities.
3. Draft project / programming specification.
4. If the system is replacing another system, will a transitional system be implemented?
5. Will the system be implemented in phases?
6. Will the system run in parallel with a legacy system?
7. Draft an impact statement which covers both personnel and information systems issues.
8. Draft a Request for Proposal if working with outside consultants or integrators.
9. Draft Project Specification if working with internal IT personnel.

PRODUCTION FORECASTS

Production forecasts are usually based on a combination of factors, including:

- Type of project
- Complexity and scale of project
- Internal resources
- Outside resources
- Previous experience

Basing production forecasts on upper management's expectations, rather than on technical manager's expertise, decreases the validity of the forecasting process and can de-motivate your technical manager.

   Accurate production forecasts enable a business to allocate resources efficient-ly. Overly conservative projections can lead to resource shortages and to reduced profitability; overly optimistic projections can lead to cash flow problems if a company acquires resources, ramps production, or increases overhead to support the optimistic production schedule.

Production Schedule

TASK MANAGER (Lead): *Philip White*

PROJECT DESCRIPTION (Primary Objective):
Enable customers to use our Internet server to track their open orders in our Order Entry system.

MILESTONES (Key Results)	COMPLETION DATE
1. User Requirements Analysis	June 1, 1997
2. Initial Product Specification	July 15, 1997
3. Approval for Specification	July 31, 1997
4. Begin Programming	August 1, 1997
5. Beta Test Interface	November 1, 1997
6. Documentation Review	November 15, 1997
7. Final Product Test	December 20, 1997
8. Implement Pilot Project	January 15, 1998
9. Announce New Capability	January 15, 1998

SCHEDULED PROJECT COMPLETION DATE: *November 20, 1997*

MANAGEMENT APPROVAL: *Laura Black*

RECRUITING AND EVALUATING TECHNICAL PERSONNEL

IT is a people business. The ability of your IT department to support your business objectives will ultimately depend on your IT personnel's ability to imagine, articulate and deliver state-of-the-art IT systems.

The hiring process in most organizations is based on a seven-step process:

1. Define staffing objectives

2. Obtain budget approval

3. Find qualified personnel

4. Screen applicants' resumes

5. Test applicants

6. Interview applicants

7. Decision process / recommendation

DEFINE STAFFING OBJECTIVES

It is difficult to recognize high potential individuals unless you know exactly what you are looking for. Before you begin the recruiting process, you should define your "ideal" candidate's previous work experience, educational background, technical skills, personality type, and management potential. Use the Job Requirements Checklist to help you define your staffing objectives and screen potential job candidates.

Job Requirements Checklist
Educational Background
•   High school
•   College / Graduate school
•   Technical / Trade school
•   Professional certification / Training
•   Sales support training
•   Other
Work Experience
•   Knowledge of specific applications
•   Experience with specific development tools and environments
•   Operating systems experience
•   Local Area Network experience
•   Wide Area Network experience
•   Communications experience
•   Intranet and Internet experience
•   User support experience
•   Specific industry experience
•   Other
Professional Skills
•   Verbal skills
•   Writing ability
•   Foreign languages skills (oral / written)
•   Technical skills
•   Analytic skills
•   Organizational skills
•   Office skills
•   Computer skills
•   Other

continued . . .

Job Requirements Checklist
Management Skills
• Technical management experience
• Product management experience
• IT Department management experience
• Other management experience
• Previous P&L responsibility
Personal Traits
• Honesty
• Loyalty
• Work ethic
• Persistence
• Confidence
• Intelligence
• Creativity
• Problem solving abilities
• Empathy / listening skills
• Professional appearance
Other Qualifications
• Desire to travel
• Conversational skills
Relevant Hobbies (Example: Cryptography)
• Other
• Other

OBTAIN BUDGET APPROVAL

An employee requisition form is often used to facilitate the hiring approval process.

Employee Requisition
Department: Research and Development
Position: Senior Programmer / Analyst
Responsibilities: Interface existing financial systems to our Internet server. Requires knowledge of C++, JAVA, Microsoft's Windows Open Services Architecture, Active-X, Windows/NT and Internet Information Server. It would be very helpful if candidate has had previous experience working with complex, Windows-based financial applications.

Status:
   • <u>Full Time</u> (PREFERRED STATUS)
   • Part Time
   • Independent Contractor
   • <u>Contract Hire</u>
   • Other:

Salary / Compensation: Depends On Experience Approved: $64,000.00 plus moving expenses as required.
Manager / Lead: Tom Brown

Recruitment Process
   • In-House Transfer:
   • Referral By:
   • Advertisement (Local / Regional / National) Source: Seattle Times Classified Ad
   • Employment Agency:
   • Corporate Search Firm: Acme Personnel

Approved By: Date:
Date Position Filled:
Human Resources:

FIND QUALIFIED PERSONNEL

The best place to find technical personnel is often within your own organization. Personnel in areas, such as support, training and customer service often have many of the skills, and a great deal of the industry and product knowledge that are key to success. If you must go outside of your company to recruit technical personnel, you can do your own search, or you can retain outside help.

If you do your own search, inform all of your business contacts that you are looking for someone to fill the position. Most companies advertise open positions in employee newsletters, on a bulletin board in the lunch room or other "visible" place, on an electronic bulletin board or Web server, or through e-mail. Employees both past and current, customers, suppliers, and industry consultants are all good referral sources.

Advertising in local newspapers, as well as in industry trade publications, is another great way to find qualified candidates. The more general your advertisement, the more resumes you will generate. If you have very specific requirements, include them in your ad. The extra money you spend advertising will reduce your screening time by pulling better qualified applicants.

You can also use outside employment agencies and professional recruiters. Free employment agencies are sponsored by government organizations, and by high schools, colleges, and private trade schools. Paid employment agencies typically collect resumes, and build an "inventory" of job seekers, by placing vague, but compelling advertisements in newspapers.

An employment agency can save you a great deal of time by screening its job applicants. Some agencies do a good job; others, however, will send over any "warm body" that is available.

Some recruiters specialize in finding technical IT personnel; however, the more specialized your job requirements, the less likely that a professional recruiter will have the technical background needed to screen candidates effectively.

Executive search firms, or "head hunters" who contract with your company to perform an exclusive job search, are usually the most professional and provide the best service. However, professional recruiters work on commission, and often charge 30 to 80 percent of a candidate's yearly salary. Because of their expense, these firms are usually retained to recruit senior technical personnel.

SCREEN APPLICANTS' RESUMES

The next step in the hiring process is screening applicants' resumes. A resume should specify educational background and previous work experience, and should provide some indication of what type of position the candidate is seeking.

Companies that receive very large numbers of resumes often use automated Document Management Systems and workflow automation to help them manage the recruiting process.

TEST APPLICANTS

Testing job applicants is a critical step in the hiring process. Most IT managers develop a series of technical questions and sample problems to evaluate how much experience and expertise an applicant has with specific applications or development environments. Whenever possible, test questions should require applicants to use their problem solving skills.

Depending on the specific skills needed, it may be helpful to retain an outside agency to administer standardized proficiency tests.

INTERVIEW APPLICANTS

Interviewing job applicants is an art. Although most managers strive to be as objective as possible, it is important to use intuition as well as intellect when selecting employees.

Whenever possible, you should interview prospective employees at least two times. First impressions are very important and can be very revealing about a prospective employee's character; but it is easier to assess qualities in another person after you are familiar with his or her personal presentation style.

Questions Which Reveal Character
• What products, applications, support services, etc., were you responsible for on your last job?
• Did you have any direct reports in your last job?
• What did you like most about your last job?
• What did you like least about your last job?
• Why do you think that working here will be a better opportunity for you?
• What were your most important achievements in your last job? Why were they important to you?
• What was your greatest business challenge? What did you learn from it?
• What was the most difficult problem you encountered? How did you handle it?
• Who was the most difficult person to work with at your last job? How did you overcome this problem?
• What was the most important course or project that you completed in school? Why was it important to you?
• Why do you think someone with your experience should be chosen for a job that requires (fill in your own job requirement) experience?
• What are you looking for in a new job opportunity?
• Convince me that you have what it takes to do this job!
• How much money did you make on your last job?
• What percentage of your salary was directly tied to performance bonuses?

If you ask each candidate you interview the same questions, your hiring process will be more objective, and it will make it easier for you to evaluate and compare different candidates that you screen over a period of time.

THE DECISION PROCESS / JOB OFFER

If you are interviewing several candidates, you can save time by creating a form to record your impressions, and by writing down your comments right after your interview while they are fresh in your mind.

PICKING WINNERS

There are many factors that determine whether a technical person will be successful in a new job: personality, maturity, previous experience, technical ability, communication skills, organizational skills, level of expectation for compensation, and other "success factors." You can create a Success Factor Matrix to help you determine whether your candidate is well suited to your specific situation.

Decision Matrix Factors 1 = low 5 = high	Candidate 1	Candidate 2	Candidate 3
Knowledge of Development Tools	3	4	5
Previous Relevant Experience	3	4	4
Demonstrated Ability to Bring Projects in on Time and Within Budget	4	2	3
Communication Skills	4	3	2
Attitude	4	4	4
Salary Requirements	4	3	2
Other Requirements			
Comments	Least technical, best communicator most management experience - highest salary	Good balance of technical and communication skills - least real world experience	Most technical. Weak communication skills. Very nervous about contacting previous employer

Success Factor Matrix	Candidate's Profile
Company Size / Culture	• Likes informal environment • Enjoys support and structure of large company
Products	• Likes working with established products • Challenged by complex / emerging technologies
Development Cycle	• Enjoys product development • Enjoys product maintenance • Enjoys product support
Compensation	• Security oriented - wants high hourly salary • Motivated by bonuses based on performance and stock options
Potential for Advancement	• Wants management experience / opportunities • Career programmer / engineer / analyst
Level of Supervision	• Needs close supervision • Likes to work alone • Wants to work at home • Wants to be a consultant
Personal Needs	• People oriented • Task oriented

All offers of employment should be made in writing, and should specify particular job requirements, reference your organization's personnel manual, describe employment compensation and benefits, and indicate any special conditions of employment, such as probationary employment periods.

New Hire Danger Signals
• If you have any concern about a candidate's honesty you should pass on the application. A candidate who lies and profits will be motivated to lie again.
• A candidate with poor verbal skills may not be able to work well with other people.
• A candidate who has had many jobs in a short period of time (unless just out of school) may not have chosen the right career path, or may be burned out.
• A candidate who asks you not to check references may have had serious problems with the last employer, may have a substance abuse problem, or may have had difficulty getting along with coworkers.
• A candidate who is very concerned about "low" compensation, but is willing to take your job anyway, may have lied about prior salary, or may leave as soon as a better paying job becomes available.
• A candidate who requires a period of time off when first hired may have personal problems, or may feel burned out from the last job.
• If you really don't like someone, don't hire that person. It is far easier to help someone you like become successful, than to spend extra time helping someone you don't enjoy being around.

EVALUATING TECHNICAL PERSONNEL

The key to evaluating technical personnel is focusing on definable contributions that are of value to the organization. For example:

- Delivering projects on time and within budget
- Helping coworkers achieve their objectives
- Quality user support
- Self-motivated to learn new skills
- Involvement with work-related professional societies
- Working independently and conscientiously

PERFORMANCE APPRAISAL

The performance appraisal process is a key factor in motivating employees, building company loyalty, and leveraging individual employees' contribution to your organization. The most effective way to implement a performance appraisal is to integrate the appraisal process with the objectives and key results that you have defined with your team members. For example, you might agree with a programming manager to base 70% of a performance rating and bonus on "delivering projects on time and within budget."

Formal performance reviews provide an opportunity for a manager to review how successful an employee has been at achieving objectives, and for the employee to describe any achievements and discuss special or corrective actions that he or she is taking to reach objectives in the future. If employees' compensation and other rewards are tied to performance appraisal, they will take the process very seriously.

Performance review meetings often begin with a tense atmosphere. The employee's performance is in fact being "judged" by the manager. The atmosphere should be as relaxed as possible to facilitate an open dialog.

If there is a disagreement between a manager and the employee on how well the employee has met objectives (performance), the manager may need to use conflict-resolution skills to move the meeting forward. In any event, the manager and the employee should each include their meeting notes in the employee's file.

Since a key objective of the employee review process is to improve the employee's future performance, there is nothing to be gained by demoralizing an employee during the performance review. This meeting should provide an opportunity for the manager to use praise and constructive criticism to help shape the employee's future behavior.

Most organizations schedule performance reviews every six months. By scheduling frequent "checkpoints" you can minimize differences of opinion on performance, productivity and the need to meet future objectives. The process typically takes one to two hours, including 30 to 90 minutes for the meeting and 20 to 30 minutes to document the meeting for the employee's file. In any case, allow enough time to review your employee's achievements, and to define objectives and key results for your employee's next appraisal period.

Performance Review Worksheet
Date: December 11, 1997
Employee: Nathan White
Supervisor: Tom Brown
Job Title: Project Manager

continued . . .

Performance Review Worksheet

Job Standards:

- Manage documentation for system users.

- Manage in-house documentation personnel.

- Review and edit all documentation developed by internal personnel.

  We expect our documentation materials to be comparable in format and presentation to materials supplied by IBM or Microsoft.

  We expect our documentation personnel to maintain quality standards which are consistent with our objective of becoming ISO 9000 certified.

  We use the Advanced Documentation Management System to produce all manuals and brochures.

Specific (Quantifiable) Objectives for This Review Period

- Hire documentation specialist for new Internet project.

- Review ISO certification requirements.

- Draft a report to COO on your department's ability to comply with these requirements.

- Redesign style guide for in-house training materials.

General (Qualitative) Objectives for This Review Period

- Meet production schedules for all materials.

- Support programming staff as required.

- Support Help Desk as required.

- Provide guidance to documentation personnel.

- Schedule weekly one-on-one meetings with all documentation personnel.

- Manage documentation issues with outside consultants and independent contractors.

Performance Rating (Rate employees in each area from 1 to 5.)

1. *Training Period*: This rating is used for employees that require additional training or experience to meet expected performance standards.

continued . . .

Performance Review Worksheet

2. *Marginal Performance:* This rating is used for employees whose performance requires some improvement to meet expected performance standards.

3. *Average or Expected Performance:* This rating is used for employees whose performance meets expected performance standards.

4. *Exceptional Performance:* This rating is used for employees whose performance occasionally exceeds expected performance standards.

5. *Performance Above Job Classification:* This rating is used for employees whose performance consistently exceeds expected performance standards. Employees with this rating are usually being groomed for promotion.

• Quality of Work	3
• Production Level	3
• Technical Skills	4
• Interpersonal Skills	3
• Organizational Skills	3
• Planning Skills	2
• Personal Development	2
• Training / Education	3
• Leadership	4
• Management Skills (Leads or Managers)	4

Major Strengths / Abilities

- Excellent leader.
- Good technical skills.
- Enthusiastic.

Significant Contributions / Improvements

- Responsible for releasing Version 2.0 of our in-house System User Guide.
- Provided backup Help Desk support.

continued . . .

Performance Review Worksheet

- Helped programming staff document user requirements for planned Internet interface to order entry system.

- Hired new documentation specialist to work on Internet project.

Improvement in These Areas Will Improve Your Overall Performance

- Planning skills are weak.

- May benefit from taking a course on "managing the planning process."

- Need to take time to grow industry skills - specifically on Internet publishing

Additional Factors Considered in Overall Performance Rating

- Consistently put in overtime during last phase of Help Desk implementation project.

- Was gone for three weeks of training at Microsoft's offices in Redmond, Washington.

Overall Performance Rating (1 to 5)   3

Performance Incentives / Bonus for This Review Period

Bonus = $3,500

Cost of living raise = 2%

New salary = $52,700 per year.

Objectives and Key Results for Next Review Period
(Specify revisions to current objectives and key results.)

- Implement HTML-based online documentation for Internet server.

- Review ISO 9000 requirements with senior management and begin developing a plan to move towards certification.

- Maintain current budget levels for department.

continued . . .

Performance Review Worksheet
Manager's Comments • *You are doing a very good job. We appreciate the work that you do, and the positive attitude that you maintain when you are on the job.* • *You need to work on your planning skills - this will help you interface more effectively with other departments, and better manage your department's budget.* • *You have done an excellent job recruiting personnel - keep up the good work.*
Employee's Comments
Manager's Signature / Date
Employee's Signature / Date
Senior Manager's Signature / Date

Many organizations have employees submit a self-evaluation form to their manager prior to their performance review.

Employee's Self-Evaluation
Date: *December 11, 1997*
Employee: *Nathan White*
Supervisor: *Tom Brown*
Job Title: *Project Manager*
Areas of Greatest Strength or Improvement: • *Stay on top of projects until they are completed correctly.* • *Good people skills.*

continued . . .

Employee's Self-Evaluation

Significant Contributions:

- Completed Version 2.0 of In-house System User Guide.

- Provided backup Help Desk support.

- Helped programming staff document user requirements for Internet interface to order entry system.

- Hired documentation specialist to work on Internet project.

- Installed file server to store all documentation on-line.

Areas Which Need Improvement:

- Our group does not have a good record of completing large projects on time. We need to specify more frequent milestones, and to be better disciplined about not changing direction once we get started.

- I am having difficulty convincing our Controller that our department's computer hardware requirements need to be prioritized.

- If we do not have a server in place by next month, our Internet documentation project schedule will slip. I would like to put this on our interdepartmental staff meeting's agenda.

Future Business / Career Objectives:

- I would like to move into product development next year. I would find it very challenging to have responsibility for creating a new training product.

- I realize that I need to have additional product planning experience before I will be ready for this type of assignment.

Employee's Comments:

- I am enjoying working with our outside contractors; they have been very professional and have delivered their work on time, and in good shape. I think I have done a good job of managing this relationship.

continued . . .

Employee's Self-Evaluation
• I would like an opportunity to take some additional management training classes to improve my personal skills.   • I have signed up for a public speaking workshop which meets on Tuesday evenings. I hope this will help me become a better communicator.
Employee's Signature / Date: How do you feel about the Performance Review Process?
Manager's Signature / Date
Senior Manager's Signature / Date

LEGAL RESPONSIBILITY

Employers are required to follow all government employment regulations. "Intent" to follow a law is no protection against legal action.

- *Job Descriptions*

  Written job descriptions which include detailed job requirements as well as a description of job responsibilities and authority should be maintained by your Human Resources / Personnel Manager.

- *Individual Assignments / Objectives*

  A copy of each employee's objectives and key results should be included in the employee file.

- *Performance Review Forms*

  Most companies use standard employee review forms to help them meet EEOC requirements, and to help them avoid litigation in case of employment policy audits which may occur if employees feel that their rights are being violated.

  Signed performance review forms should be maintained in the employee's file.

- *Job Standards*

  Most companies document organizational and departmental standards and policies, as well as system development standards and policies.

  For example, your company may require employees to maintain computer passwords, or to use a specific program development methodology.

CHAPTER 11

MANAGING AND TRAINING TECHNICAL PERSONNEL

Senior management's primary IT challenge is recruiting the best IT personnel available, and providing them with continuing education opportunities to ensure that the organization stays abreast of emerging technologies. In addition to these factors, management can eliminate a great deal of unnecessary work, and develop positive attitudes by providing:

- Realistic priorities

- Realistic project deadlines

- Adequate staff and budgets

- Well defined job responsibilities

- Adequate project planning

- Necessary access to corporate resources

MOTIVATING TECHNICAL PERSONNEL

Many senior managers are intimidated by IT professionals because they do not understand new technologies, and because they have not learned how to communicate effectively with the people who do. But companies that lock away their technical personnel in a "back room," are putting their company at risk. Technical people need support and encouragement like any other employees. Failure to provide this can lead to the loss of key personnel, and to expensive employee turnover.

Technical personnel are motivated by a variety of rewards, including money, job security, recognition, intellectual challenge, the opportunity to work with new technologies, working facilities, their relationships with their peers, and their relationship with their manager. With the exception of a fascination with emerging technologies, technical personnel are motivated by the same factors as other employees.

MANAGING TECHNICAL WORKGROUPS

Being part of a technical workgroup is very different from being part of a traditional workgroup. While the latter typically focuses on individual achievement, the former must focus on achieving the team's goals. In technical workgroups, less senior professionals often have more technical expertise than their managers' and no individual has hiring, firing, or rewarding "power" over anyone else.

Different people on technical projects often report to managers in different business units, such as their organization's technical support and application development groups. So their workgroup is really a functional rather than an organizational unit.

Technical personnel must cooperate, and rely on group collaboration to achieve their goals.

Old Workgroup Management Philosophy	New "Team" Management Philosophy
People feel that work is inherently unpleasant	People enjoy working as much as playing if their work environment is supportive and positive
People are inherently lazy and irresponsible	People want to do a good job, and will accept responsibility if they are capable, and motivated
People lack creativity	People are creative if given the chance to participate in the planning process
People must be motivated by external forces, such as money and fear of losing their jobs	People are motivated by internal factors, such as a need for acceptance by their coworkers
People must be closely controlled and supervised to accomplish their jobs	People are self-directed, and can motivate themselves to succeed if provided adequate incentives

THE DELEGATION PROCESS

Delegating work can help you save time in two ways. First, if you have too much work to handle yourself, you can spend more of your time on high level analysis and problem solving by delegating work to others; second, delegation provides an opportunity for you to empower and develop the people that work with you.

- *Select the Best People for Your Team*

  Recruiting the best people that you can find is the best prescription for a successful team.

  Don't assume that an employee who has been doing one job for a long time cannot do other more demanding tasks. Average workers who are given greater responsibility are often capable of delivering outstanding results.

- *Don't Overload Your Best People*

  Try to assign tasks to other people that have not yet had an opportunity to reach their peak level of performance.

- *Define Your Delegation Goals*

  Take the time to determine which tasks you can delegate, and which tasks you want to be involved with.

  Unless you take the time to delegate specific types of work to specific personnel, you will have to assign each task on a case-by-case basis.

- *Delegate Tasks to Your Suppliers*

  Many suppliers are pleased to provide "free" services to help them win future business. You can often "leverage" your suppliers to help you define user requirements, analyze interoperability issues, and provide product information.

- *Communicate Clearly*

  Communicate the task (assignment) that you are delegating to your coworker or assistant as clearly and precisely as you can.

- *Include Your Client's Personnel and Your Coworkers in the Planning Process*

  By including them you can help them learn new skills and take "ownership" of their delegated tasks.

Include Clients in Your Planning Process
• People are more committed to projects that they help plan themselves
• People get a greater sense of accomplishment by doing work that they helped plan
• There is better communication when everyone is involved from the planning stage

continued . . .

Include Clients in Your Planning Process
• People are more supportive and cooperative when they feel like equal team members
• The work process can often be shortened by involving clients in the planning process
• It is easier to spot problems early on, rather than after your project is underway
• Your clients (and coworkers) may have different ideas about how to accomplish a task taking the sum of everyone's experience will help ensure the best plan is adopted

- *Assign Simple Tasks to Less Experienced Personnel*

  As you become more confident of your coworkers' skills, you can assign them more complex tasks and grant them greater authority to act.

- *Negotiate Deadlines*

  Whenever possible, you should discuss deadlines with the people that you are delegating work to, and confirm that they can get their assigned tasks done in a reasonable period of time.

- *Rotate Assignments*

  Challenge yourself to not favor people that you like with the best opportunities. Some of the most successful technical people are difficult to get along with. Rotate assignments between your coworkers so that they don't get "burned out," and so that each worker has the opportunity to learn new job skills.

- *Delegate Problems to Less Experienced Team Members*

  Whenever practical, senior people should delegate problems to less experienced team members and then serve as mentors to build experience within their group.

  Try to delegate tasks to individuals at the lowest level in your organization that have the information, capabilities, and judgment to fulfill the task.

- *Don't Abdicate Responsibility for Critical Tasks*

  If you are in doubt about a delegated task being completed properly, and on schedule, you should remain involved until it is completed. The alternative may be to spend the same amount of time managing your stress!

- *Follow Up on All Assignments*

  Don't abdicate responsibility for assignments that you delegate. Stay in contact with your coworkers to ensure that their tasks are on track, and on time.

- *Don't Take Back Assignments*

  Micro-managing or taking back assignments wastes your time and your coworker's time. Try to use "problem" situations as training opportunities.

- *Make All Criticism Constructive*

  Demoralized employees do not do better work.

- *Give Your Coworkers Latitude to Take Initiative*

  Give your coworkers the latitude to get tasks done their way, so that they can learn to exercise their initiative and creativity.

  Inexperienced managers believe that their job responsibilities confer an inherent right to support from their coworkers. Professional managers know that they must earn their coworkers' support.

- *Reward Successful Efforts*

  Behavior that is rewarded persists. If your coworkers do a good job, you should reward them with praise, special recognition, the opportunity to work on more advanced jobs in the future, and financial remuneration.

Tips for Effective Delegation
• Delegates must be capable and motivated
• Training leverages performance
• Verify communication and confirm deadlines
• Establish checkpoints and provide guidance
• Be positive and implement rewards
• Don't "micro-manage" or take back delegated tasks

- *Master of Their Domain*

  Egocentric, technically insecure and emotionally immature IT personnel can put their organization at risk.

  Egocentric technical personnel, for example, may perceive their organization's operations to be revolving around "their" IT infrastructure, in contrast to a less egocentric, and more realistic view of the IT department's role as a support and service organization.

IT managers that have weak management skills, or are technically insecure, can "engineer" reliance on their technical expertise by not documenting applications or support processes, by not providing systems level documentation, and by not encouraging cross-training to eliminate the risk of losing essential information if they or other key IT personnel become unavailable.

- *Why Don't They Document Their Code?*

It is human nature to enjoy some tasks more than others. For example, most software engineers prefer developing new code to maintaining code that another engineer has developed. Similarly, most programmers prefer to write code, than to document the code they write.

Most programmers are convinced that they write "great code" that any other "smart" programmer can understand and maintain. In reality, undocumented code is extremely difficult to maintain as a business's needs change over time.

If senior management is not confident that mission-critical systems are adequately documented, it should hire outside consultants to audit the documentation, and if necessary, hire technical writers to help internal personnel document their work.

If documentation continues to lag new product development, management can mandate that mission-critical projects be documented *before* any new projects may be started. This sounds Draconian, but it is very hard to motivate programmers and systems analysts to change bad habits.

Senior managers should insist that all of their mission-critical systems are documented, and that their IT personnel are cross-trained to engineer "survivability" into their information systems infrastructure.

Delegation Planner
PROJECT: Select PC vendor for Intranet Server
DATE: August 15, 1997
ASSIGNED TO: Tom Sander

continued . . .

Delegation Planner
LEAD / MANAGER: Philip White
PRIORITY: <u>A</u>   B   C
DO BY: Time: _____ / Today / This Week / <u>This Month</u> / This Quarter
OBJECTIVES: Evaluate and select a PC supplier to host our Intranet server. System must support multiple Intel Pentium Pro processors, and be compatible with Windows/NT Internet Information Server. We prefer to work with one of our existing suppliers, unless there is a compelling reason to work with a new supplier.
AUTHORITY LEVEL • Act, no report necessary. • Act, report if unsuccessful or if more time is needed. • <u>Recommend action to manager.</u> • Bring information to manager.
ACCOUNTABILITY KEY RESULTS: Complete evaluation within two weeks. CHECKPOINTS: Review report with manager before submitting report to IT manager. DUE DATES: Submit report with recommendation by September 15, 1997.

MANAGING WITH OBJECTIVES

Working with your staff to define objectives is a great way to improve communication and develop more supportive relationships; and using key results to measure performance can help objectify employee reviews, and improve decision making[18] Two types of objectives can be used to focus your employees' efforts: *qualitative* objectives, such as "improve communication skills," and *quantitative* objectives, such as "design 25 new management reports."

---

[18] Source: This section has been adapted from *Selling Microsoft,* Doug Dayton, 1997, Adams Publishing.

Nine Steps to Defining Objectives and Key Results	**Example**
1. Define Your Goals	Develop a new Intranet-enabled order entry application for the telemarketing group.
2. Define Your Key Results	Prototype user interface with Visual Basic. Develop RDBMS links. Test application with Web browser. Implement application on internal Intranet.
3. Evaluate Your Strengths and Weaknesses	Have extensive systems analysis skills and programming experience. Our programmers have completed Java training, but they have never created an Intranet-hosted application.
4. Budget Your Resources (Time, Personnel and Capital)	Team has 1 month to design the application. We will budget $2,500 for outside consulting if needed. Team has 14 weeks to program and test the application.
5. Determine a Course of Action	Two programmers are scheduled to attend an Intranet workshop. Our team leader will work with our sales manager to define user requirements.
6. Determine Completion Date	We will have the project completed by August 15th.
7. Write Down Your Plan	Each team member has a written action plan.
8. Monitor Results	I will track my team's progress with an on-line project management system.
9. Implement Rewards	Our entire team will go on a paid holiday to Nothing Much To See if we complete our work on schedule.

1. DEFINE YOUR GOALS

Before you can define your goals, you must determine what your "mission" is. The easiest way to define your mission is to ask yourself the question: "What am I trying to accomplish?" For example, your goal might be to install and implement an Intranet application.

Before committing yourself to attaining a goal, you should evaluate whether the goal is achievable and challenging. Goals that cannot be achieved are de-motivating; and goals that are not challenging will not help you improve your productivity.

2. DEFINE KEY RESULTS

Next, you should define the performance criteria, or key results, that you will use as milestones to help you define progress towards your goal. They should provide an objective measure of your progress towards your objectives. For example, to achieve an objective of implementing an Intranet application, you might need to purchase hardware and software, and complete a specialized training program.

3. EVALUATE YOUR STRENGTHS AND WEAKNESSES

Once you have determined what your goals are, and you have defined your key results, you are ready to analyze your strengths and weaknesses to determine whether you have all of the resources, including time, personnel, equipment and capital that you will need to attain your objectives.

Evaluating your strengths and weaknesses is often the most difficult phase of the planning process, because you rarely have all of the information that you need to be certain that your analysis is complete and accurate.

You may, for example, not know how long it will take to evaluate firewalls from different suppliers, or not know how long it will take your team to develop and test a complex business object. The important thing is to be honest and realistic, and to use all of the information that you have to help you anticipate what you will need to do to reach your objectives.

4. DETERMINE A COURSE OF ACTION

At this point, you should be ready to develop an action / development plan that describes how you will achieve your objectives. The key to creating an effective plan is to evaluate each activity that you are involved with, and then to prioritize the activities that you want to focus on to help you attain your key results.

5. DETERMINE A COMPLETION DATE

Defining completion dates for each activity that you have planned provides an opportunity to test your conviction that you can achieve your key results by a specific date, and provides an opportunity to evaluate the relative priorities of different tasks.

6. Budget Your Resources (Time, Personnel, Equipment and Capital)

After you have put together your action / development plan, you will need to budget the resources that you are going to use to accomplish your activities. If, for example, your objective is to implement an Intranet application, you may need to budget time to attend an Intranet security seminar, meet with hardware and software suppliers, and review published product evaluations.

7. Write Down Your Plan

There are three key reasons why it makes sense to write down your plan.

- The process of writing down your action / development plan can help you evaluate your plan's logic.

- Having a written action / development plan makes it easier to communicate your ideas with other people.

- Having a written action / development plan can help you stay focused on the activities that are most important to reaching your goals.

8. Monitor Your Results

You should review your progress towards attaining your objectives at frequent enough intervals to take corrective action, if you begin to miss your key results. If this occurs, you will need to re-evaluate your plan to determine whether you still believe that it will enable you to attain your objectives. If you no longer think so, you will need to re-prioritize your activities, or develop an entirely new plan. For example, if you are having difficulty evaluating "firewall" software, you may need to hire an outside consultant to help you review your options. Most technical specialists review their progress towards achieving their key results with their manager on a weekly or biweekly basis.

9. Implement Rewards

Incentives, such as money and personal recognition, motivate people to perform as well as they can. The more desirable an incentive, the more motivating it is. A $5,000 bonus is, for example, much more motivating than an overnight trip to Nothing Much To See.

> When you introduce the concept of management by objectives to your staff, you should focus on achieving your team's most important goals. If you try to accomplish too much, or if you try to track too many objectives and key results, you will waste time and overwhelm your staff.

TRAINING IT PERSONNEL

Investing in training and certification programs will help ensure that your technical personnel maintain their professional skills, and will help reduce employee turnover.

Most companies send their technical personnel to at least one training program each year. Depending on the needs of the organization and the individuals' skill level, they may attend academic courses, professional seminars, technical workshops or conferences. Technical workshops are often the most effective because they involve participants, and provide an opportunity to try out new skills. The main problem with workshops, however, is that the technical problems which are studied are artificial—real world situations are usually much more complex.

In addition to these "formal" learning opportunities, technical personnel should be encouraged to develop their professional skills through self study. Many companies, for example, reimburse their employees for technical books and publications that they purchase to stay abreast of emerging technologies.

> Invest in training to leverage the productivity of your personnel and to reduce installation, implementation and maintenance costs.

TRAINING REQUIREMENTS

Most organizations have a broad range of training requirements, including:

- *Systems Architecture and Design*

  IT personnel should be trained on both legacy and emerging technologies.

- *Application Program Development*

  IT personnel should learn new programming tools and application design methodologies.

- *System Support and Maintenance*

  IT personnel should attend vendor training on hardware and operating systems level products which have been installed, or are being evaluated for adoption.

- *Mission Critical Application Support*

  IT personnel should attend vendor training on mission critical applications, to enable them to provide first level user support.

- *Office Tools (e.g.: office application suites, e-mail, groupware)*

  IT personnel should be trained on office applications to enable them to provide first level user support.

- *End-User Computer Training*

  End-users should be trained on office tools, and on all mission-critical applications.

- *Company Policies and Procedures*

  All personnel should attend in-house training on IT policies and procedures such as those related to system security.

TRAINING PLAN

The IT manager should develop a training plan that covers the breadth of skills necessary to make the organization as self-sufficient as possible.

In most organizations, the Human Resources department must rely on the expertise of the IT manager to identify specific training requirements for IT personnel, and all system users.

Sample Training Requirements Plan for Implementing an Enterprise Wide Web (Intranet)

- Introduction to Networking and TCP/IP
- Building HTTP Web Pages
- Building and Maintaining a Web Site
- Microsoft Windows NT Server Certified Professional Classes
- Microsoft Internet Information Server Training
- Designing and Publishing Forms on the Internet

Sample Training Requirements for System Users

- Basic PC Skills
- Introduction to the Internet
- Introduction to Internet Tools
- Using Microsoft Office and Electronic Mail
- Publishing Information on the EWW

12

WORKING WITH CONSULTANTS

Most organizations retain IT consultants to help manage peak work loads, provide specialized technical expertise, and provide objectivity and perspective.

- *Peak Loads*

  When your IT personnel cannot complete required projects on time, it may be necessary to hire outside consultants or "sub-contractors" to enable you to complete your tasks.

- *Technical Skills*

  If your IT personnel do not have specific technical skills, such as connecting your LAN to the Internet, it may be more cost effective to use an outside consultant rather than to develop that expertise in-house.

- *Objectivity / Perspective*

  IT personnel are often convinced that the systems and methodologies that they are most familiar with are the best, when in fact this may or may not be the case. Outside consultants can provide an objective reality-check on IT plans, and can bring a fresh perspective to complex IT problems.

OBJECTIVES AND DELIVERABLES

Before hiring a consultant, you should develop a detailed project specification or "scope of work" which defines your objectives and deliverables. The better defined your project, the easier it will be for your consultant to stay focused, the easier it will be for you to manage the work, and the less chance you will have of litigation arising from misunderstandings.

Many organizations attach a detailed project specification as a work definition to their consultant's service agreement.

IT CONSULTANTS

IT consultants generally provide one of two types of services or deliverables: *implementation* services and *advisory* services. Implementation services consist of developing, installing, implementing and maintaining IT systems and applications. Advisory services include analysis, training and recommendations on current IT strategies and methodologies, and on specific IT products.

Consultants that provide implementation services may have a conflict of interest if they also provide advisory services. For example, consultants retained to do a search for an accounting application will tend to be biased towards those accounting applications that their company is authorized to resell. Consultants that do not provide implementation services would be less likely to be biased.

Therefore, as a rule, you should not hire any advisory consultant who sells or represents any IT products or support services, or has any other conflict of interest. Your consultant's only "interest" should be your success.

EVALUATING CONSULTANTS

It can be very difficult to evaluate a consultant's expertise and competence because there is not always a good correlation between technical competence and "salesmanship." Great technologists often have poor interpersonal skills; conversely, technical personnel with great personalities and communication skills are often poor technical performers.

- *Technical Expertise*

  Consultants have diverse technical backgrounds. Some consider themselves "specialists," and focus on a specific area, such as writing device drivers for hardware peripherals. Others are "generalists," and may, for example, work on any financial application developed in COBOL. Most development managers consider themselves to be generalists and have worked on a broad range of projects at some point in their career.

  Depending on the work that you need done, you may need to retain one or more specialists or generalists. In any case, it is wise to verify before work begins that your consultant has whatever expertise is necessary to complete your project. Otherwise, you may wind up paying for a consultant's education on your time.

- *Communication Skills*

  It is important to select a consultant that has good interpersonal skills. They must work effectively with clients that they have literally just met, and over whom they have little or no corporate influence.

- *Referrals*

  Referrals from other clients are often the best way for you to assess a consultant's capabilities. In most cases, referrals for projects similar to the work that you are contracting will be the best predictor of competence.

  Before you hire any outside consultants—regardless of your confidence in their capabilities—you should check their credentials and references, and protect yourself with a written contract.

- *Size of Consulting Firm*

  Larger consulting firms can usually provide technical specialists with a broader range of skills than smaller firms, and can schedule as many specialists with specific technical experience as necessary to meet tight production schedules.

  Larger consulting firms usually have more experience managing and delivering large projects than smaller firms. However, smaller consulting firms can often provide better response time; moreover, they will often assign more senior technical personnel to your project than larger consulting firms, which often use smaller projects as training opportunities for less experienced personnel. Smaller firms are also usually less expensive than larger firms, in part because they have less management overhead.

- *Fixed Price vs. Time and Materials Contracts*

  Some consultants will offer fixed price contracts based on their estimate of how long it will take to complete your project. Other consultants are only willing to take work on a time and materials basis.

  Fixed cost contracts minimize your financial exposure; however, they do not guarantee that your project will be completed on time, or that your work will be done correctly.

  Some consultants will put in as much time as necessary to completely satisfy their client, while other consultants' primary objective is to maximize their profit by providing as little work as possible to satisfy their client's work order.

FINDING THE RIGHT CONSULTANT

The best sources of consultants are referrals from business colleagues and from companies that have sold you IT equipment and services.

If your industry and professional business contacts cannot help you locate a qualified consultant, you should check advertisements in regional computer newspapers, and in your local telephone directory under Data Processing, Computers or Business Consulting Services.

INTERVIEWING CONSULTANTS

Interviewing a prospective consultant is just as challenging as interviewing a prospective employee for your company. During your interview, you will need to evaluate both your consultant's technical expertise and interpersonal communication skills.[19]

You will also need to determine whether the consultant is a good fit for your project. The best way to determine this is to provide as much information as possible about the scope of your project. Communicate any expectations that you have about development methodologies, documentation, project milestones, status meetings, and, of course, your expected time for completion of the work.

WHEN CONSULTANTS SHOULD "JUST SAY NO"

Experienced consultants will turn down work if:

1. They do not feel that they have the technical skills to complete the job.

2. They are concerned about a personality conflict with one or more individuals in their prospective client's organization.

3. They are concerned about being "micro-managed," or are uncomfortable having frequent status meetings with their client.

4. They do not believe that their prospective client understands the scope of the task, and they don't want to argue about it with them.

5. They are not interested in the project because of the development tools being used, the platform that is being targeted, or the development methodologies their prospective client has adopted.

6. They do not think the project will be as profitable as another opportunity.

---

[19] You can use the suggestions in Chapter 2, Recruiting and Evaluating Technical Personnel, to help guide your interview process.

Many organizations team internal personnel with outside consultants so that they can bring the consultants' expertise into their organization.

REQUEST FOR PROPOSALS (RFPS)

The best way to articulate the scope of your project and any special requirements that you have is to create an RFP. When competing consulting firms respond to your RFP, you can evaluate their approaches to addressing your needs, and you can get a better idea of how much your project is going to cost, and how long it will take to complete.

CONSULTING AGREEMENTS

A written business agreement is the best way to clarify a business relationship. A Professional Services Agreement can help you avoid misunderstandings, and is invaluable if you ever need to seek legal remedies.

Both the sample Professional Services (Consulting) Agreement and the Acknowledgment of Independent Contractor Status and Assignment of Rights are intended to serve as a general guideline for developing your own agreements. *You should consult with your attorney before drafting or signing any legal agreements.*

PROFESSIONAL SERVICES AGREEMENT

Agreement made (Date) , 199X, between _____, a (sole proprietorship / partnership / corporation) organized and existing under the laws of the State / Province of _____, with its principal place of business at _____, herein referred to as Client, and The Consulting Firm, a (sole proprietorship / partnership / corporation) with its principal place of business at (Consulting Firm's Address), herein referred to as Consultant.

RECITALS

- Client desires Consultant to perform consulting services as specified in Appendix A.

  Attach Appendix A to your contract and have both parties initial and date the page.

  The more specific your description of services (deliverables) is, the clearer your agreement will be.

- Client agrees to make its personnel and resources available as necessary to complete the services specified in Appendix A.
- Consultant agrees to perform these services for Client under the terms and conditions set forth in this Agreement.

I. PLACE, TIME AND STATUS OF WORK

- It is understood that Consultant's services will be rendered largely in (City, State), but that Consultant will, on request, come to the Client's address or to such other places as designated by the Client to meet with its representatives.
- The number of hours Consultant is to work will be approved in advance by Client and mutually agreed to by Consultant. The hours Consultant is to work on any given day will be entirely within Consultant's control and Client will rely upon Consultant to put in such number of hours as are reasonably necessary to fulfill the spirit and purpose of this Agreement.
- Neither Consultant nor any of Consultant's staff is or shall be deemed to be employees of Client. Consultant shall be responsible for ensuring that Consultant's employees or sub-contractors are competent to perform work for Client.
- Each party agrees that while performing services under this agreement, and for a period of six months from completion or termination of this agreement, neither party will, except with the other party's written agreement, solicit or make any offer of employment to any of the other party's employees or sub-contractors.
- Consultant and Client agree that Client shall have the non-exclusive ownership of any applications, software, documentation, other deliverables, or ideas embodied therein, that are described in Appendix.
- Client agrees to nominate one individual as its primary contact with Consultant. (Enter Contact's Name) is authorized to represent Client during performance of this agreement with respect to the services and deliverables defined in Appendix A, and has authority to execute written modifications and additions to this agreement.
- If Client wants to modify the scope of this agreement as defined in Appendix A, Consultant may at its sole discretion agree to make such modifications, or may terminate this agreement if Consultant believes that the changes are outside the scope of its expertise. If Consultant agrees to make such modifications, Client agrees to pay Consultant additional consulting fees, based on Consultant's daily or hourly consulting rate.

II. PAYMENT

- Client agrees to retain Consultant for a minimum of ___days, or for additional hours/days as mutually agreed by Client and Consultant.

- Client will pay Consultant $ _____ (US) per day, or $ _____ (US) per hour, of Consultant's time used in the performance of services under this agreement.

- Client will reimburse Consultant for all long-distance telephone calls, computer time, supplies, and any other expenses incurred in the performance of services on Client's behalf.

- Travel time will be billed at one-half of Consultant's daily/hourly consulting rate. Travel time will be considered billable time if Consultant is required to travel more than 20 miles from (City, State). Air travel will be billed directly (when possible) to Client.

- The responsibility to provide consulting services will be accepted and work will begin when Consultant receives a non-refundable retainer of $ _____ (US). Once this initial advance has been exhausted, Client agrees to pay Consultant the total balance due pursuant to the Consultant's invoice.

- Client will pay invoices for consulting services within fifteen days of receipt of Consultant's invoice. Overdue invoices will be charged a 5% late fee and 1.5% per month interest.

OR

Client agrees to pay Consultant for Consultant's services as specified in Appendix B.

Attach Appendix B to your contract and have both parties initial and date the page.

III. CONFIDENTIAL AND PROPRIETARY INFORMATION

Each party acknowledges and agrees that any and all information concerning the other's business is "Confidential and Proprietary Information," and each party agrees that it will not permit the duplication, use or disclosure of any such "Confidential and Proprietary Information" to any person (other than its own employee, agent or representative who must have such information for the performance of its obligations hereunder), unless such duplication, use or disclosure is specifically authorized by the other party. "Confidential and Proprietary Information" is not meant to include any information which, at the time of disclosure, is generally known by the public or any competitors of the parties to this Agreement.

IV. INDEMNIFICATION

The Client does hereby indemnify and shall hold harmless (including reasonable attorneys' fees) the Consultant against all liability to third parties (other than liability solely the fault of the Consultant) arising from the performance of consulting services under this Agreement. Client's obligation to indemnify Consultant will survive the expiration or termination of this Agreement by either party for any reason. Client may, at its option, conduct the defense in any such third party action arising as described herein and Consultant promises to cooperate fully with such defense.

V. LIMITATION OF LIABILITY

Consultant's nonperformance shall be excused if caused by equipment failure, acts of God, strikes, equipment or facilities shortages, or other causes beyond Consultant's reasonable control. In addition, Consultant's liability, if any, for any mistake, omission, interruption, delay, error, defect or other failure in its recommendations or delivery of service or equipment, whether in contract, tort, strict liability or otherwise, shall in no event exceed the amount of Consultant's contract. In no event shall Consultant be liable to Client for any amount arising out of or connected with this agreement (except as specifically set out in the previous sentence) or for any costs, delays, special, incidental or consequential damages. In the event that this limitation of liability is held unenforceable, parties agree that Consultant's liability will be limited to $100.00 (US) as liquidated damages, and not as penalty.

VI. MISCELLANEOUS

- Either party to this Agreement may terminate this Agreement by giving 10 days notice to the other party.

- Notices to Client should be sent to: _____

  Notices to Consultant should be sent to: _____

- Consulting fees for any work that has been completed prior to notice of termination will be paid within fifteen days of receipt of Consultant's invoice.

- Any modifications or addendum to this contract shall only be made in writing.

- If either Client or Consultant employs attorneys to enforce any rights arising out of or relating to this Agreement, the prevailing party shall be entitled to recover attorneys' fees and any costs of collection.

- This Agreement shall be governed by the laws of the state of (State).

IN WITNESS WHEREOF, the Parties hereto have executed this Agreement as of the day and year first above written.

CLIENT BY: _____ DATE_____

TITLE: _____

CONSULTANT BY: _____ DATE_____

FOR: The Consulting Firm

ACKNOWLEDGMENT OF INDEPENDENT
CONTRACTOR STATUS AND ASSIGNMENT OF RIGHTS

1. Independent Contractor Status: I, _____ acknowledge and agree that I am performing the services required by this Independent Contractor Agreement as an independent contractor of (Client's company) , and not as Client's employees.

2. Assignment of Rights: I assign to (Client's company) my entire right, title and interest (including all copyright and patent rights) in all copyrightable or patentable inventions, discoveries, improvements, innovations, ideas, designs, drawings, computer programs, computer code or writings produced or created by me as a result of, or related to, performance of work or services under this Independent Contractor Agreement. This assignment is effective as of the date of the creation of any protectable works created under this Independent Contractor Agreement.

I will cooperate with all lawful efforts of (Client's company) to register and enforce this assignment. I shall execute and aid in the preparation of any papers that (Client's company) may consider necessary or helpful to obtain or maintain any patents, copyrights, trademarks or other proprietary rights at no charge to Consultant, but at its expense. (Client's company) shall reimburse me for reasonable out-of-pocket expenses incurred.

3. Confidentiality: I acknowledge that all information and materials I may acquire about Client's business is Client's confidential and proprietary information. I agree during and after the term of this Independent Contractor Agreement to hold such confidential information in strict confidence. I will not disclose Client's confidential information to anyone other than employees or agents of Consultant working on this project who must have such information to perform Consultant's obligations under this Independent Contractor Agreement unless I obtain Client's prior written authorization. Upon Client's request, I will promptly return to Client all originals and copies of all documents, records, software programs, media and other materials containing any confidential information of Client.

Subcontractor:

Signature: _____ Date: _____

Accepted by (Client's company):

By:_____ Date: _____

CALL TO ACTION!

"The convergence of data processing and telecommunications is bringing about fundamental changes in our social and economic structures, and with them new business opportunities. Electronic delivery systems open a broad range of substitution possibilities, including electronic funds transfer systems, office automation, and electronic publishing. For businesses, competitive success will depend more and more on identifying substitution possibilities, resegmenting markets, and deploying the technology in new ways in production, marketing, distribution, and research and development. For consumers, the new technology means better use of personal time and resources, greater educational opportunities, and improvements in the quality of life."

"As full electronic transaction capability becomes more economically plausible for business and home, the possibility arises that a significant part of what today involves for example "going to the office," and "going shopping" can be accomplished from any place where there is a terminal."[20]

This quote is from a talk presented by John Diebold at a meeting of Diebold Group, Inc. clients in Chicago, Illinois on April 25, 1980. Mr. Diebold delivered this talk *before* the PC Revolution, *before* the LAN revolution, and *before* the business world became aware that the Internet existed.

Mr. Diebold's speech is as relevant today as it was prescient over sixteen years ago. By paying attention to innovations in computing, communications, and systems management, Mr. Diebold was able to anticipate the impact of widely available computing resources and high-bandwidth network computing on business and society.

Every company that tracks emerging technologies can put itself in a position to realize a competitive advantage by becoming an early technology adopter. But taking this step has risks. As we have discussed, organizations should only adopt new technologies when their potential for increasing revenues, decreasing expenses and addressing new business opportunities outweighs the risks.

---

[20] *Managing Information,* John Diebold AMACOM, 1985

The key to leveraging your IT systems as a competitive tool is being able to *visualize* the impact that emerging technologies will have on your fundamental business model, and then positioning your business to *adopt* those technologies as soon as they are mature enough to help your business achieve a competitive advantage.

EVERYTHING CHANGES BUT THINGS STAY THE SAME

Over the last twenty years, IT managers have moved from centralized mainframe platforms, to decentralized client-server platforms, to re-centralized network computing platforms. Despite these paradigm shifts, senior management's expectations for IT have remained virtually unchanged.

A 1994 *Datamation* magazine survey confirmed that IT managers are primarily concerned with improving productivity, aligning IT with their organization's business strategies, improving quality of service and reengineering business processes. But IT systems today still do not support pervasive computing, achieve complete interoperability or provide maximum usefulness. And many organizations will need to replace or reengineer their IT infrastructure to prepare their organization for the impact that "next-generation" network computing technologies will have on their fundamental business model.

IT Management's Major Activities	Critical	Very Important	Somewhat Important	Not Important
Improve Productivity	42	47	11	0
Reengineer IT to Align with Company Strategy	35	38	13	13
Improve Quality	32	54	14	0
Reengineer Business Processes	32	38	22	8
Reduce IT Costs	17	33	36	14
Improve Competitive Advantage	13	38	22	27
Create Information Architecture	11	47	30	11

continued . . .

IT Management's Major Activities	Critical	Very Important	Somewhat Important	Not Important
Implement Emerging Technologies	8	53	31	8
Sell IT to Senior Management	8	47	30	16

DEVELOPING AN EFFECTIVE INFORMATION RESOURCE MANAGEMENT STRATEGY

Aligning IT strategies to support your business objectives is a major challenge, but it can be achieved if you have a clear understanding of your business objectives, your legacy systems, and emerging technologies.

- *Gather Information*

  The easiest way to learn about emerging technologies is to read magazines, such as *Information Week* and *Datamation,* which publish articles targeted to senior managers.

  When you read about an emerging technology which may be of value to your organization, think about how it may impact your business model if and when it becomes widely adopted.

- *Track Strategic Technologies*

  It is virtually impossible to keep up with all of the advances, announcements and product introductions which are fueling the Information Revolution. Fortunately, there are five heuristics that you can use to help you identify which technologies are most likely to impact your organization.

  1. *Track technologies that can lower the cost of maintaining your current information systems.*

     For example: many companies are replacing proprietary minicomputers with PC-based servers to reduce their operating costs.

  2. *Track technologies which enable your organization to reengineer business operations.*

     For example: many companies are deploying collaborative workflow applications to enable them to reengineer their business processes and lower their operating costs.

3. Track technologies which enable interoperability between different types of systems.

For example: PC-based computer telephone integration (CTI) solutions are revolutionizing the PBX market.

4. Track technologies which simplify IT interfaces.

For example: many companies are adopting the Lightweight Directory Application Protocol to facilitate interoperability between disparate network applications.

5. Track technologies which drive new computing and communication standards.

For example: emerging technologies such as Digital Subscriber Lines will ultimately define high-bandwidth, wide area network communication standards.

- *Establish a Formal Technology Evaluation Program*

In large organizations, the chief information officer is usually responsible for identifying and evaluating emerging technologies. In smaller companies, a manager from IT or finance is usually the best resource for this task.

In the past, chief information officers were recruited from academic environments and from leading system integration companies. Today, most CIOs are promoted from within their organization, after developing the business acumen they need to understand and articulate the strategic value that their organization's information systems can provide.

- *Leverage Internet Technologies*

As network computing builds momentum, there is a "once-in-an-IT-paradigm-shift" opportunity to leverage interest in the Internet.

Your organization can use this excitement to help it sell the IT budgets necessary to achieve pervasive computing, interoperability and maximum usefulness.

- *Initiate an Information Technology Audit*

Your organization can use the business and information systems audit worksheets in this book to help you align your IT infrastructure with your strategic business objectives, and to help you assess the potential impact of emerging technologies.

- *Elevate Technology to Your Board Room*

Senior managers should make their Board of Directors aware of the impact that emerging computer and communication technologies may have on their fundamental business model.

If emerging technologies require your company to reengineer your operations to remain competitive, you will need your Board's support.

ACHIEVING SUCCESS

Most businesses do not know how much impact their information systems have on their bottom line. If they did, senior management would devote more time to understanding and managing the company's IT resources. By taking a few hours each week to learn about emerging information technologies, and to contemplate how they may be of value to your organization, you can begin "reinventing" your business to meet the challenges of the Information Revolution. Reinventing your business will take some time—but as you begin deploying new technologies, you will quite literally "reengineer" your success.

INDEX

A

Access logs, 177
Accountability of IT systems, 177
Advertising to find qualified personnel, 221
Application design review for technological innovation, 166
Application metering, 200-202
Application Programming Interface (API), 161
Architecture of evolving systems, 11-32
    bandwidth, 27
    breakpoints, 16-17
    client-server computer model, 21
    computing trends, future, 28-29
    convergence, 25
    data management trends, future, 32
    data mining, 24
    data storage, 12
    Digital Video Disk (DVD), 12
    document management systems (DMS), 14-16
    ergonomics, 13
    Ethernet protocol, 19
    future computing trends, 28-29
    future network trends, 29-32
    Internet (World Wide Web), 22-27
        (*see also* Internet)
    LAN Revolution, 18-19
    market demand as driving force, 27-28
    microprocessors,11-12
    network computing, 22-25
    networking trends, 19, 29-32
    Online Analytic Processing (OLAP), 24-25
    page scanners, 13, 14
    PC Revolution, 18
    peripherals, 13
    rapid application development (RAD) tools, 13
    recentralization, 21-22
    remote access computing, 21
    software, 13
    year 2000 problem, 28
Asset inventory, 148-49
Asymmetric cryptosystems, 179
Audit and requirements planning, difference between, 3
Auditability of IT systems, 177
Auditor, selecting, 3-4
    notes of, 34
    recommendation of, 113-14

B

Bandwidth, 27
Baseline budgeting, 193
Breakpoints, 16-17
Budget approval for hiring personnel, 217, 219-20
Budgets, IT, 191-202
    acquisition costs, 198-200
    analyzing, 96-97
    assumptions, four, 191
    baseline, 193
    cost control, 196
    funds, allocating, 193-96
    incremental, 192
    items to include, 193
    as management tool, 191
    presentation, 197
    process, 192-93
    selling, 197-98
    software licensing, 200-202
        Concurrent Licenses table, 201
    zero-base, 192-93
        decision packages, 192

263